THE SUBLIME

Often labelled as 'indescribable', the sublime is a term that has been debated for centuries amongst writers, artists, philosophers and theorists. Usually related to ideas of the great, the awe-inspiring and the overpowering, the sublime has become a complex yet crucial concept in many disciplines. Offering historical overviews and explanations, Philip Shaw looks at:

- the history of the sublime from the earliest, classical theories, through those of the Romantic era, to post-modern and avant-garde conceptions of sublimity
- the major theorists of the sublime such as Burke, Kant, Lyotard, Derrida, Lacan and Žižek, offering critical introductions to each
- the significance of the concept through a range of literary readings including the Old and New Testaments, Homer, Milton and writing from the Romantic era
- how the concept of the sublime has affected other art forms such as painting and film, from abstract expressionism to David Lynch's neo-*noir*

This remarkably clear study of what is, in essence, a term which evades definition, is essential reading for students of literature, critical and cultural theory.

Philip Shaw is senior lecturer in English Literature at the University of Leicester.

THE NEW CRITICAL IDIOM

SERIES EDITOR: JOHN DRAKAKIS, UNIVERSITY OF STIRLING

The New Critical Idiom is an invaluable series of introductory guides to today's critical terminology. Each book:

- provides a handy, explanatory guide to the use (and abuse) of the term
- offers an original and distinctive overview by a leading literary and cultural critic
- relates the term to the larger field of cultural representation.

With a strong emphasis on clarity, lively debate and the widest possible breadth of examples, *The New Critical Idiom* is an indispensable approach to key topics in literary studies.

Also available in this series:

THE SUBLIME

Philip Shaw

Routledge
Taylor & Francis Group

LONDON AND NEW YORK

First published 2006
by Routledge
2 Park Square, Milton Park, Abingdon, Oxon OX14 4RN

Simultaneously published in the USA and Canada
by Routledge
270 Madison Ave, New York, NY 10016

Reprinted 2008

Routledge is an imprint of the Taylor & Francis Group

Typeset in Garamond and ScalaSans by
Taylor & Francis Books
Printed and bound in Great Britain by
Antony Rowe, Chippenham, Wiltshire

British Library Cataloguing in Publication Data
A catalogue record for this book is available from the British Library

Library of Congress Cataloging in Publication Data
A catalog record for this book has been requested

ISBN10 0–415–26847–8   ISBN13 9-780-415-26847-8 (hbk)
ISBN10 0–415–26848–6   ISBN13 9-780-415-26848-6 (pbk)

T&F informa

Taylor & Francis Group is the Academic Division of T&F Informa plc.

For Betty and Olive

CONTENTS

SERIES EDITOR'S PREFACE

The New Critical Idiom is a series of introductory books which seeks to extend the lexicon of literary terms, in order to address the radical changes which have taken place in the study of literature during the last decades of the twentieth century. The aim is to provide clear, well-illustrated accounts of the full range of terminology currently in use, and to evolve histories of its changing usage.

The current state of the discipline of literary studies is one where there is considerable debate concerning basic questions of terminology. This involves, among other things, the boundaries which distinguish the literary from the non-literary; the position of literature within the larger sphere of culture; the relationship between literatures of different cultures; and questions concerning the relation of literary to other cultural forms within the context of interdisciplinary studies.

It is clear that the field of literary criticism and theory is a dynamic and heterogeneous one. The present need is for individual volumes on terms which combine clarity of exposition with an adventurousness of perspective and a breadth of application. Each volume will contain as part of its apparatus some indication of the direction in which the definition of particular terms is likely to move, as well as expanding the disciplinary boundaries within which some of these terms have been traditionally contained. This will involve some re-situation of terms within the larger field of cultural representation, and will introduce examples from the area of film and the modern media in addition to examples from a variety of literary texts.

ACKNOWLEDGEMENTS

Numerous friends and colleagues have assisted in the preparation of this book. I wish to thank, in particular, Tom Bristow, Michael Davies, Emma Kimberley, Sarah Knight, Anshuman Mondal, Vince Newey, Mark Rawlinson, and Peter Spratley for their comments and advice. I am grateful to Douglas Burnham and to Michael John Kooy for their help with Kant and to Nick Everett and Alison Morgan for the extended book loans.

Philip Shaw, September 2005

INTRODUCTION

The sublime is not so much what we're going back to as where we're coming from.

(Nancy 1993: 1)

WHAT IS THE SUBLIME?

Derived from the Latin *sublimis*, a combination of *sub* (up to) and *limen* (lintel, literally the top piece of a door), the sublime is defined by the *Oxford English Dictionary* as 'Set or raised aloft, high up' (see Wood 1972). The word has many applications. A building or a mountain may be sublime, as may a thought, a heroic deed, or a mode of expression. But the definition of the sublime is not restricted to value judgements; it also describes a state of mind. The cavernous interior of St Paul's Cathedral instils a sense of awe; King Lear's dying words fill the audience with lofty emotion; the idea of infinity is beyond words.

Our attempts to match such grandeur necessarily fall short of the mark. How, for example, should we speak of God? In Psalm 139, David proclaims that divine knowledge 'is too wonderful' to express; 'it is high, I cannot attain it' (line 6; *Holy Bible* 2001). Yet somehow a sense of God's majesty is conveyed through this very failure. And it is not only the elevated or pleasing that inspires such thought. The *OED* goes on to describe the effect of the sublime as crushing or engulfing, as something we cannot resist. A revolution, for instance, may be sublime in so far as it carries a people along with it, inspiring them with grand ideals, convincing them that the world can begin anew. To some, the imagining of apocalypse is sublime. What could be loftier and at the same time more terrifying than the revelation of St John? For the critic James Usher, writing in the late eighteenth century, the power of the sublime is such that it 'takes possession of our attention, and all our faculties, and absorbs them in astonishment' (Ashfield and de Bolla 1996: 147). Most recently and most controversially, those of us who looked agog at the destruction of the twin towers on September 11 2001 could be said to have experienced something of this power to astonish (see Žižek 2002), a claim to which I will return in chapters 6 and 7.

In broad terms, whenever experience slips out of conventional understanding, whenever the power of an object or event is such that words fail and points of comparison disappear, *then* we resort to the feeling of the sublime. As such, the sublime marks the limits of reason and expression together with a sense of what might lie beyond these limits; this may well explain its association with the transcendent, conceived by the theologian John Milbank 'as the absolutely unknowable void, upon whose brink we finite beings must dizzily hover' (2004: 211). The sensation of cognitive failure in the face of the sublime is evoked by the Romantic poet John Keats (1795–1821) in his poem 'On Seeing the Elgin Marbles', composed in 1817:

> My spirit is too weak – mortality
> Weighs heavily on me like unwilling sleep,
> And each imagined pinnacle and steep
> Of godlike hardship tells me I must die
> Like a sick eagle looking at the sky.
> Yet 'tis a gentle luxury to weep
> That I have not the cloudy winds to keep
> Fresh for the opening of the morning's eye.
> Such dim-conceived glories of the brain
> Bring round the heart an undescribable feud;

So do these wonders a most dizzy pain,
That mingles Grecian grandeur with the rude
Wasting of old time – with a billowy main –
A sun – a shadow of a magnitude.

(Keats 1978)

In Keats' vision, knowledge is no longer present as a 'peak' to be scaled and conquered by the questing mind. The object of the poet's attention, the recently appropriated Pantheon marbles, is 'dim-conceived' and 'undescribable' (*sic*). Yet the collapse of the marbles into fragmentary images and shards of broken syntax has the curious effect of conveying a sense of power and majesty beyond the reach of understanding. Once again, descriptive failure raises a negative, even painful, presentation of the ineffable.

Sublimity, then, refers to the moment when the ability to apprehend, to know, and to express a thought or sensation is defeated. Yet through this very defeat, the mind gets a feeling for that which lies beyond thought and language. A moment ago I suggested that the concept of the sublime lends itself well to the idea of the transcendent, whether encountered in the Hebrew Bible or in the poetics of Romanticism. Yet such instinctive feeling for the transcendental is rare these days. As a result of secularism, together with increasing global awareness and media sophistication, we seem less inclined to regard the breakdown of reason and expression as indicators of a higher or spiritual realm. Thus, as the critic Thomas Weiskel has claimed, even as the sublime continues to bear on our imaginative life, we no longer share in the sacred or mystical aspects of the sublime, which went unquestioned by previous generations (1976: 36).

The postmodern sublime, one might say, is defined not by its intimations of transcendence but rather by its confirmation of immanence, the sense in which the highest of the high is nothing more than an illusion brought about through our misperception of reality. As the postmodern theorist Slavoj Žižek has written, 'in art the spiritual and material spheres are intertwined: the spiritual emerges when we become aware of the material inertia, the dysfunctional bare presence, of the objects around us' (2003: 13–14). For example, in a scene from David Lynch's film *The Straight Story* (1999), the camera focuses on the view from an ordinary suburban window frame; the indifference of the scene is disturbed by the entrance of an orange ball rolling from right to left. The film makes no attempt to explain this event; the ball is just a ball, yet in its detachment from any form of context (Where did it come from? Why is it here? Where does it go?), the image becomes invested with significance beyond its 'dysfunctional bare presence'. For Lynch, the moment when the world is shown to be blank, mute, and absurd is far removed from the expressive vitality of the Hebrew psalms. If this is indeed a spiritual moment, it is one that emerges at precisely the point when all that we know, all that we have felt, thought, and understood, becomes useless, or even ridiculous (see Žižek 2000b). On this understanding, the sublime experience points no longer to an object *beyond* reason and expression, but rather to 'that *within* representation which nonetheless *exceeds* the possibility of representation' (Milbank 2004: 212). Uncoupled from the Judeo-Christian concept of the divine, the sublime is figured in postmodern thought as immanent rather than transcendent.

We will go on to explore the consequences of this shift in understanding in the following chapters. For now, it may be that these thoughts have already overreached themselves, so much so, perhaps, that they have become a demonstration of the very thing I am attempting to describe: an experience that is excessive, unmanageable, even terrifying. With this in mind, let us turn now to a brief account of the history of the sublime.

THE SUBLIME HAS A HISTORY

Since the concept was first presented in the *Peri Hupsos* or *On Sublimity* (1965), an aesthetic treatise attributed to the Greek critic Dionysius Longinus in the first century CE, the sublime has stood, variously, for the effect of grandeur in speech and poetry; for a sense of the divine; for the contrast between the limitations of human perception and the overwhelming majesty of nature; as proof of the triumph of reason over nature and imagination; and, most recently, as a signifier for that which exceeds the grasp of reason. Common to all these definitions is a preoccupation with struggle: for Longinus, the discourse of the sublime, whether in political oratory or in epic verse, works to overcome the rational powers of its audience, persuading them of the efficacy of an idea by means of sheer rhetorical force. In Longinus' view, as we shall see in chapter 1, listeners and readers are ravished or, more disturbingly, raped by the power of words.

The rhetoric of violence also pervades the religious writings of Thomas Burnet (1635–1715). In his *Telluris Theoria Sacra* (1680–9, translated into English as *The Sacred Theory of the Earth*, 1684–9; see chapter 2), Burnet envisions the day of judgement when the enemies of God, terrified by his unspeakable Glory, 'call for the Mountains to fall upon them' (1965: 302). Published in the wake of the first widely available text of *Peri Hupsos*, translated as *Traité du Sublime* by Despréaux Boileau in 1674, *The Sacred Theory of the Earth* locates the sublime within the context of the biblical apocalypse. Although the work makes no direct reference to Longinus, its concern with the grandeur and power of the divine, contrasted with the limits of sinful nature, feeds directly into writings on the sublime dating from the eighteenth century. With particular focus on the writings of John Dennis, Joseph Addison, and Lord Shaftesbury, we will look at how speculations on sublimity prompt anxieties about the self, the nature of the divine, and the ethics of nobility.

Burnet's work is important additionally for its analysis of the origins of the sublime. Whilst Longinus stresses sublimity as a purely rhetorical phenomenon, Burnet and his followers in the eighteenth century pay close attention to the vast and grand in nature. As the literary critic Marjorie Hope Nicolson (1959) has argued, interest in the 'natural sublime' initiated a major shift in British culture as poets and artists turned from the representation of politics and manners towards the exploration of mental and physical intensity. The lofty mountain peak or the swelling ocean, as depicted in the poems of Akenside and Thomson, and in the writings of the Romantics, discussed in chapter 5, thus became the scene for darker meditations on the nature of the self and its relations with the external world (see Hipple 1957).

The emphasis on the pleasure and pain of sublime experience, evident in the literature of this period, owes much to the influence of the Irish politician, aesthetician, and pamphleteer Edmund Burke (1729–97). As in Burnet's writings, the threat of violation is a constant theme in Burke's. In his landmark *A Philosophical Enquiry into the Origin of our Ideas of the Sublime and the Beautiful* (1757; 1990), however, the threat of violence is mitigated by the effects of distance: an erupting volcano may well induce terror in the mind of one about to be engulfed by lava, but to the distant spectator the sight could be experienced as a form of delight. In this secularised version of Burnet's apocalypse, the viewer may exercise a facility for aesthetic contemplation; the volcano is judged not to be a threat to life and is perceived instead as an example of the awesome destructive power of nature. Through repeated exercise, the meeting with the sublime strengthens our powers of conception; we become, as it were, equal to the powers we survey.

Drawing on the legacy of the Longinian tradition, Burke directs his analysis towards the effects of the sublime in language. It is at this point, as many recent critics have noted (see de Bolla 1989; Ferguson 1992), that the *Enquiry* begins to expose a fault line in the history of the sublime. Words have a power, Burke argues, to raise the idea of the sublime, such that the distinction between the sublime object and its description no longer applies; it is language, in other words, that brings about the transformation of the world, enabling us to hymn the vastness of the cathedral or the depths of the ravine. More radically, the stress on sublimity as an aspect of language leads Burke to undermine the privileging of human consciousness. For if the grandeur of the ocean is no more than a matter of rhetoric or description, might the same not be said of other alleged truth claims, such as the integrity and autonomy of the self?

For the German philosopher Immanuel Kant (1724–1804), in an extension of this thought, the struggle is between the evidence of the senses (what philosophers refer to as the empirical domain) and the supersensible power of reason (literally over or above sense). Here, as I argue in chapter 4, the sublime affirms ultimately the ascendancy of the rational over the real: the mind of man, that is, is greater than anything that might be discovered in nature (see Kant 1789; 1987). With Kant and his followers in the German Idealist tradition of philosophy, the emphasis shifts decisively away from empiricist or naturalistic theories of the sublime and towards the analysis of sublimity as a mode of consciousness. Yet here again, as the poststructuralist theorists Paul de Man, Jacques Derrida, Philippe Lacoue-Labarthe, and Jean-François Lyotard have argued (see chapter 6), there are critical indicators in

Kant's text that the analysis of the sublime reveals the failure point of idealism, highlighting the dependency of consciousness on the transformational power of language.

Though Derrida, de Man, and Lyotard display scepticism towards the Kantian tradition, they nevertheless continue to work within its parameters. And the same is true of their contemporaries working in the spheres of art and literature. If the tone of the so-called 'postmodern sublime' is less positive, less routinely convinced of the transcendental significance of the sublime, its meanings and structures continue to be informed by the findings of the past. In the work of the American abstract painter Barnett Baruch Newman (1905–70), for example, a yearning for transcendence is pitted against an open acknowledgement of the impossibility of this desire. The sublime emerges in Newman only as an instant of creative intensity, derived not from God, nature, or indeed from mind, but rather from the event of artistic creation. The sense of the beyond, that is, is nothing other than an effect of oil on canvas.

An engagement with the constructed nature of the sublime is evident in the work of Mariele Neudecker (1965–). Drawing on the rich legacy of German Romantic painting, Neudecker's meticulously crafted dioramas, housed in water-filled vitrines, invite the viewer to enter into a world of hidden depths and seemingly infinite space, only to dispel the pleasure of this engagement through the recollection of its underlying deceit. Neudecker's emphasis on the melancholic tone of the postmodern sublime, a melancholy prompted by the shattering of illusions, is evident also in the titles of her works, such as *Unrecallable Now* (2001) and *Over and Over, Again and Again* (for further discussion see Brown and Young 2004).

The work of the postmodern architect Daniel Liebeskind (1946–) is similarly fêted for its preoccupation with the impossibility of representation, in this case of failing to convey the enormity of human experience, whether conveyed in the broken corridors and sealed spaces of the Berlin Jewish Museum or, more recently, in the controversial designs for the Twin Towers memorial. For Liebeskind, the sublime emerges in moments of blockage and frustration; it is an architecture that gestures towards the absence of something much greater. Although clearly indebted to the theories of Derrida and Lyotard, the emphasis in such work on the elegiac, the disrupted, and the monstrous draws on currents in the discourse of the sublime that go back to Longinus, Burke, and Kant.

In light of these examples we might wish to regard the postmodern sublime as an attempt to re-read a theoretical tradition, placing emphasis on its paradoxical, unfulfilled, or self-baffling emphases. Recalling Žižek's comment, quoted earlier, if there is a spiritual dimension to the postmodern sublime, it resides in the ability of contemporary culture to negate the material inertia of things in such a way that it allows us to come alive to the feeling of something beyond the merely functional or utilitarian. Such a feeling might emerge, for instance, when surveying the material vacancy of the art of Andy Warhol (1928–87). The Marilyn Monroe series prompts the viewer to meditate on the relentless drive of capitalist reproduction but in a way that forces us to become aware of its inertia, its still point. The Marilyn portrait is iconic, in the religious sense, because no amount of reproduction can nullify its enigmatic presence. We might say that Warhol's art is sublime despite itself. And such a feeling can take the viewer by surprise.

Perhaps there is nothing new about this feeling. When, in 1798, the poet William Wordsworth (1770–1850) referred to the deep, underlying significance of things as

> a sense sublime
> Of something far more deeply interfused,
> Whose light is the dwelling of setting suns,
> And the round ocean, and the living air,
> And the blue sky, and in the mind of man,
> A motion and a spirit, that impels
> All thinking things, all objects of thought,
> And rolls through all things ...
>
> (Wordsworth 1984)

it is the effort to overcome the recalcitrance of words, their resistance to the elevated, which most impresses. Wordsworth, perhaps more than any other poet, is profoundly aware of the gulf separating thought and expression. The most important words are not, as we might expect, the words of manifest greatness or power, such as 'suns', 'air', and 'ocean', but rather those words which in ordinary language hardly merit attention, words such as 'and', 'all', and 'in'. The poem's use of connectives ('And the round ocean, and the living air, / And the blue sky …') is an attempt to compensate for the material deadness of words, to make the connection between objects and ideas. Wordsworth's lines encompass that 'something' which lies beyond the reach of human comprehension yet somehow, miraculously dwells '*in* the mind of man' (see Wlecke 1973).

Even so, there are important distinctions to be made in the developing meaning of this concept. Part of the function of the following chapters is to show readers how the theories of Longinus, Burnet, Burke, Kant, Lyotard, Derrida, and Žižek differ from each other. Whilst it is possible to point to structural similarities between, say, the Romantic and the postmodern ideas of the sublime, we should be no less aware of their key dissimilarities. In the case of Lyotard, as we shall discover, the goal of the sublime is to sustain a sense of shock, to prevent the reader/viewer/interpreter from coming to terms with the meaning of that which exceeds the norm. If the aim of Romanticism is somehow to incorporate the 'sense sublime', postmodernism, by way of contrast, seeks to retain a sense of the sublime as other, a 'something' that can never be 'interfused' through the use of metaphors, symbols, or verbal connectives. Since, as we have seen, such an approach might well usher in Romanticised notions of reverence and awe through the back door, as it were, other versions of postmodernism endeavour to do away with the sublime altogether.

Before proceeding, I wish finally to say a word about beauty. Since Burke, the concept of the beautiful has been set against the concept of the sublime, more often than not as a point of theoretical contrast. The sublime is greater than the beautiful; the sublime is dark, profound, and overwhelming and implicitly masculine, whereas the beautiful is light, fleeting, and charming and implicitly feminine. Where the sublime is a divisive force, encouraging feelings of difference and deference, the beautiful encourages a spirit of unity and harmony. In political terms, the impulse of the one, we might say, is individualistic, even dictatorial, that of the latter is social and democratic. Although theory has confined itself, for the most part, to analyses of the sublime, in recent years some attempt has been made to reappraise the beautiful, to regard it not merely as a weaker sister figure but as a just counter-spirit to the violent encroaches of the sublime. This discussion will be addressed in the afterword.

The gendered nature of the distinction between the sublime and the beautiful also has a history: in Longinus, as was noted, sublime speech 'ravishes' or rapes the listener; in Burke, the sublime is a virile masculine power, one that is contrasted with its passive feminine counterpart, the concept of the beautiful. Even more explicit in the early Kant is the distinction between the depth and profundity of the masculine sublime and the shallow, slight nature of the feminine beautiful (see Kant 1764; 1960: 46–9, 60, 78, 93, 97). In the light of this insistent distinction it will come as no surprise to learn that the concept has attracted much recent attention from feminist as well as Marxist, psychoanalytical, postcolonial, and deconstructive theorists. As Patricia Yaeger has argued, the sublime 'is ... a masculine mode of writing and relationship' (1989: 202; see also Maxwell 2001); its imprint is seen everywhere: from the elevated poetics of John Milton's religious epic *Paradise Lost* (1667) to the abyssal confrontations of Francis Ford Coppola's anti-Vietnam war film *Apocalypse Now* (1979). Feminist critiques of Longinus, Burke, and Kant, as well as more recent attempts to assert a notion of the feminine sublime, will be discussed in due course.

THE SUBLIME IS NOW

In a very strong sense the sublime does indeed verge on the ridiculous; it encourages us to believe that we can scale the highest mountains, reach the stars and become infinite when all the time it is drawing us closer to our actual material limits: the desire to outstrip earthly bonds leads instead to the encounter with lack, an encounter that is painful, cruel, and some would say comic. The sublime, somewhat ironically, given its overtly metaphysical ambitions, turns out to be a form of materialism after all. Perhaps the sublime is irony at its purest and most effective: a promise of transcendence leading to the edge of an abyss. Still, there may be a sense in which even such falls come to depend on ways of thinking that have no relation to any underlying material cause. And here is a further twist of irony: could it be that the sublime does indeed affirm the unlimited nature of being? Could the concept of the sublime, as Kant believed, lead ultimately to the triumph of mind over matter, or possibly towards an affirmation of the divine? So many questions straining towards the limits. We are never certain of the sublime.

NOTE ON TEXTS AND APPROACHES

In addition to the core texts by Longinus, Burke, and Kant, I have made extensive use of *The Sublime: A Reader in Eighteenth-Century Aesthetic Theory* (1996), edited by Andrew Ashfield and Peter de Bolla. This anthology reflects the broadly poststructuralist approach of de Bolla's earlier book-length study, *The Discourse of the Sublime: Readings in History, Aesthetics and the Subject* (1989), in which sublimity is regarded as a textual or linguistic phenomenon. Rooted in the work of contemporary French theorists, such as Michel Foucault and Jacques Derrida, de Bolla reads the history of the sublime as an increasingly sophisticated attempt to come to terms with the idea that 'there is nothing beyond the text'. In the discourse of the sublime we thus become aware that all points of origin such as God, nature, or mind are merely effects of the combinatory power of language. Over the following pages we will encounter several readings that build on this claim, substituting de Bolla's discourse with related terms such as *parergon* (Derrida 1987), rhetoric (de Man 1990), the unpresentable (Lyotard 1991), the offering (Nancy 1993), and the Thing (Lacan 1992).

De Bolla's work is, in part, an attempt to correct the more 'commonsense' assumptions of Samuel Holt Monk's classic study of the sublime. Published in 1935 (reprinted 1960), *The Sublime: A Study of Critical Theories in Eighteenth-Century England* remains an invaluable source of information. I have to some extent favoured Monk over de Bolla by maintaining the place of Kant in this tradition. Readers should also be aware of another influential early study, by Marjorie Hope Nicolson. In *Mountain Gloom and Mountain Glory: The Development of the Aesthetics of the Infinite* (1959) Hope Nicolson stresses the importance of non-Longinian approaches to the sublime. Again, readers approaching de Bolla for the first time are advised to consult this work for the insight it gives into the relations between sublimity, religion, and the limits of language.

1

BEFORE (AND AFTER) LONGINUS

ECSTASY AND INSTRUCTION

Peri Hupsos or *On Sublimity*, sometimes attributed to the Greek critic Dionysius Longinus, is widely acknowledged to be the first properly theoretical discussion of the sublime. Dating from around the first century CE, the nature and focus of *On Sublimity* is primarily rhetorical; basically it sets out to teach those oratorical devices that enable a speaker to move or persuade an audience. As such, Longinus was part of a long tradition of practical instructors going back to the Latin orator, philosopher, and poet Cicero (106–43 BCE) and linked to the republican ethos of political speech. What distinguishes *On Sublimity* from its predecessors, however, is the stress its author places on a mode of speech that is indeterminate or without form, a quality that renders the pedagogical aspect of the work extremely problematic. Whilst standard devices (see Crystal 1995: 70) such as *inventio* (the gathering of relevant subject matter), *dispositio* (the process of composition), *elocutio* (the use of rhetorical style to suit the occasion), *memoria* (the putting to memory of the various elements of the discourse), and *actio* (the delivery or punctuation of speech) could be taught and put into practice before assemblies or tribunals, the sublime seemed to elude definition. Reading *On Sublimity*, therefore, it is easy to conclude that the author secretly regards his subject as formally unteachable. Longinus' apparent stress on novelty and invention certainly chimed with the aesthetic concerns of his seventeenth-century French translator, Despréaux Boileau. As Jean-François Lyotard comments, for Boileau, 'the sublime cannot be taught … [it] is not linked to rules that can be determined through poetics'. It requires a certain 'je ne sais quoi' to detect the presence of this 'inexplicable' and 'hidden' phenomenon; it takes a 'genius' to master its use (Lyotard 1989: 201). Boileau's Baroque emphasis on the novelty and circumstance of sublime discourse continues to influence modern appropriations of his work. Thus, the English critic D. A. Russell maintains that while the work is undoubtedly a 'how to' rhetorical manual (Longinus 1964: ix), its emphasis on rote learning is qualified by a fascination with the mysterious influence of genius which 'inspires and possesses our words with a kind of madness and divine spirit' (Longinus 1965: 9). Again, the sublime is something that the elevated individual instinctively knows: one does not learn the sublime; one catches it, like a divine contagion.

In a general sense, therefore, the sublime is beyond definition; we cannot point to a rule that will govern its regulation in the same way that we can with the rhetorical devices mentioned above. What we can do, however, is point to its effects:

> For grandeur produces ecstasy rather than persuasion in the hearer; and the combination of wonder and astonishment always proves superior to the merely persuasive and pleasant. This is because persuasion is on the whole something we can control, whereas amazement and wonder exert invincible power and force and get the better of every hearer. Experience in invention and ability to order and arrange material cannot be detected in single passages; we begin to appreciate them only when we see the whole context. Sublimity, on the other hand, tears everything up like a whirlwind [or 'pulverizes all the facts like a thunderbolt'; see Longinus 1964: 62], and exhibits the orator's whole power at a single blow.
>
> (Longinus 1965: 2)

Against the standard course of rhetorical instruction, which proceeds methodically and with due care to the entire range of the work, the thunderbolt of sublimity can emerge from a single phrase. What strikes an audience with wonder (*ekplexis*) is more powerful than what merely persuades or pleases us. Unlike conventional public speech, therefore, the sublime is a discourse of domination; it seeks to ravish and intoxicate the audience so that a grand conception may be instilled in the mind without any bothersome appeal to reason or justice. As the eighteenth-century critic Thomas Reid would go on to note, 'What [Longinus] call[s] sublime in description ... carries the hearer along with it involuntarily, and by a kind of violence rather than by cool conviction' (Ashfield and de Bolla 1996: 178).

This description would suggest that the sublime is a product of nature rather than of art. Yet, as Longinus insists, although 'nature is on the whole a law unto herself in matters of emotion and elevation, she is not a random force and does not work altogether without method' (1965: 2). Feelings, in other words, may arise in nature, but art is required to give them shape and coherence. The author goes on to describe a number of devices that may be employed to sublime effect, a list that includes hyperbole, periphrasis (circumambulatory or round-about speaking), comparisons, similes, and metaphor.

The emphasis on categorisation fails, however, to elide the fundamental sense in which the sublime escapes the grasp of its teacher; one can use hyperbole, for example, without inducing the sublime, and the same is true of all the devices Longinus cites. All that remains essential to the sublime is a state of feeling, which may be loosely described as wonder, awe, rapture, astonishment, ecstasy, or elevation, terms that rest uncomfortably with the increasingly functional nature of public speech (see Auerbach 1965: 194–5), or, for that matter, with the protocols of didactic instruction.

It is in this latter respect that Longinus differs from his great Augustan precursor, the poet and critic Horace (65–8 BCE). In his verse epistle *Ars Poetica* (*The Art of Poetry*, *c.* 10 BCE), Horace lays great store on the idea of *ars* as a 'practiced mastery of craft, as a systematic knowledge of theory and technique, and as a capacity for objective self-criticism' (Leitch 2001: 122). For Horace, great thoughts and strong emotions must be subordinated to the rules of 'decorum', to 'the discernment and use of appropriateness, propriety, proportion, and unity in the arts' (123). Whilst Longinus agrees with Horace on a number of points, for example on the use of imitation, he is critical of the idea that technical accomplishment should count for all.

Longinus' criticism of the Horatian or formalist approach to literature is directed mainly at his rival Caecilius, author of an earlier, as yet
undiscovered, treatise on the sublime. Sublimity, according to Longinus'
reading of Caecilius, is equated with rhetorical excellence. But whilst a
'faultless and pure writer' such as the orator Lysias may show more decorum than the philosopher Plato, the latter, for all his faults, is more
inspired and thus more sublime (Longinus 1965: 39). For Longinus,
'intensity' is greater than sobriety, 'living emotions' are higher than
'good breeding', 'speed ... vehemence and power' compensate for lack of
'fluency, smoothness' and 'charm'. Thus the orator Demosthenes
'redeems all his mistakes many times over by a single sublime stroke'
(43). Hyperides, Bacchylides, Lysias, and Ion may be 'impeccable, uni-
formly beautiful writers' (42), but for Longinus the electric shock of
sublimity is all.

RHETORIC AND NOBILITY

A wayward genius is thus preferable to a faultless pedant. But in privileging the expression of elemental human passions Longinus does not
favour a return to aesthetic primitivism. His genius is not the wild-
eyed, raving bard of Romantic imaginings, but a cultivated, noble, and
urbane poet, aware of the distinction between the exhibition of raw,
untutored feeling and the measured expression of weighty thoughts.
Sublimity is thus 'the echo of a noble mind' and in many instances
occurs 'apart from emotion' or even 'verbal expression'. In Longinus'
view 'a mere idea' can 'sometimes be admired for its nobility – just as
Ajax's silence in the Vision of the Dead [from Homer's *Odyssey*, scroll 11.
563] is grand and indeed more sublime than any words could have been'
(1965: 9).

Longinus' interest in the sublimity of the noble mind extends, then,
even to the concealment of its slavish dependence on the materiality of
words. 'A figure', he argues, 'is generally thought to be best when the
fact that it is a figure is concealed' (26). In the treatise, this point is
exemplified in a startling analysis of the words of Dionysius the
Phocaean in Herodotus' (*c.* 480–425 BCE) *History*: 'Now, for our affairs
are on the razor's edge, men of Ionia, whether we are to be free or slaves
... so if you will bear hardships now, you will suffer temporarily but be

able to overcome your enemies.' Here, Longinus notes, the 'natural order' would have been: 'Men of Ionia, now is the time for you to bear hardships, for our affairs are on the razor's edge.' The inverted order of expression, which appears so natural, lends urgency to the situation and creates an impression of power and authority, so that the Ionians are effectively seduced into obeying the commander's will. 'The result', Longinus concludes, 'is that he seems to be giving not a premeditated speech but one forced on him by circumstances' (30).

To grant further support to his argument, Longinus looks back to ancient Greek models, in particular to Homer and the great epics, the *Iliad* and the *Odyssey* (c. 800 BCE). Key to Homer's 'pure' sublime is the sense in which rhetorical devices are effaced by the sheer power of the sublime style. As Erich Auerbach points out, however, Longinus is not averse to recasting the Iliad in order to support his theory. Thus, the passage in *On Sublimity* that reads, 'The high mountains and the wood, the peaks and the city of the Trojans and the ships of the Achaens shook beneath the immortal feet of striding Poseidon' (trans. Auerbach 1965: 225–6) is based on a conflation of *Iliad* 13 (lines 18–19) and 20 (line 60). The sentence that continues the quotation is taken from *Iliad* 13, lines 27–9: 'He guided the chariot over the waves; below him the sea monsters sprang from their clefts on all sides and recognized their lord; joyously the sea parted; but they [the steeds] surged onward ... .' According to Auerbach:

> Longinus has made the scene even more grandiose and long-rolling than it is in Homer by skipping the relatively tranquil interruption in which the palace, the horses, Poseidon's garment and scourge, are described; probably not by design but unconsciously in his enthusiasm for the sublime, he has ignored the wording, which in the first lines refers plainly to a journey on foot and in the others to a chariot ride.
>
> (1965: 226)

The ideal conception of the sublime, as presented by Longinus, is the product of a radically altered text. By omitting Homer's 'tranquil interruption', the emphasis falls exclusively on the delayed verb 'shook' in line 19 and on the rapid transition from the roused sea monsters of line 28 to the parted sea of line 29. Longinus claims that the passage 'represent[s] the divine nature as it really is, pure, majestic, and undefiled'. Yet this claim is acceptable only with the cutting of the middle lines, along with the surrounding context of the passage, referring to Poseidon's passionate enthusiasm for the Achaens and his anger against Zeus.

But there is a more serious point to make here. Earlier on in the treatise Longinus states that the orator Demosthenes conceals the figures in his speech 'by sheer brilliance. ... As fainter light disappears when the sunshine surrounds them, so the sophisms of rhetoric are dimmed when they are enveloped in encircling grandeur' (cited by Hertz 1985: 17). The method of concealment, as Neil Hertz points out, is, however, 'itself a figure, a simile using the language of light and darkness' (17). Longinus' frustration with the ineluctable materiality of language is expressed elsewhere via comparisons with the 'filthy and contemptible' nature of the body. Just as nature conceals 'the private parts' of the body, 'so as not to spoil the beauty of the creature as a whole', so sublimity works to hide its shameful dependence on the stuff of language (1965: 50). As the contemporary French poet and essayist Michel Deguy comments, this no doubt explains Longinus' enthusiasm for the silence of Ajax: a silence that is more sublime than any speech (1993: 24).

The distrust of figures may be extended to Longinus' comments on genius. Like the 'pure' divinity of Poseidon, Longinus seems to believe that 'the ideas and emotions of the genius precede ... linguistic "ornamentation"' (Leitch 2001: 137). In maintaining this view, Longinus departs again from Horace, who in the *Ars Poetica* emphasises the importance of rhetorical analysis, whilst downplaying the consideration of emotional psychology. Horace and Longinus stand, therefore, for two competing approaches to literature: on the one hand, a tradition that focuses exclusively on the intrinsic or formal aspects of texts, and, on the other, an approach that considers extrinsic or non-formal aspects. We will return to examine the problems arising from both approaches in subsequent chapters.

A further aspect of Longinus' idea of nobility requires explanation at this point. At the beginning of the treatise it is made clear that the 'public man' for whom he writes should be a man of 'worth, sincerity, and gravity' (1965: xiv). Intellectual distinction is thus related to morality. The problem is of course that sublimity tends to vitiate conventional standards of behaviour. How, for example, should we equate Demosthenes' 'violence' with the requirements of 'service and utility'? The inspired genius ravishes his audience; how can he also raise them up? The relation between sublimity and the erratic and ungovernable force of literature remains problematic, therefore. This relation also raises a question mark over its political worth. Can the domineering aspects of sublimity co-exist with democratic notions of justice, truth, and fairness?

Longinus does, however, insist that sublimity has an ethical dimension. Whilst in conventional terms it may be better to act as well as to write free from 'blame' (42), the risk-taking impulse of the sublime preserves a social function. Towards the end of the treatise, for example, Longinus lends his concept to a mordant denunciation of what is a precursor of commodity culture, with its emphasis upon desire, acquisition, and pleasure:

> But I wonder whether what destroys great minds is not the peace of the world, but the unlimited war which lays hold on our desires, and all the passions which beset and ravage our modern life. Avarice, the insatiable disease from which we all suffer, and love of pleasure are our two slavemasters. ... Avarice is a mean disease; love of pleasure is base through and through. I cannot see how we can honour, or rather deify, unlimited wealth as we do without admitting into our soul the evils which attach to it.
>
> (52)

As the echo of a noble mind, the sublime elevates man above the tawdry concern with wealth and status. However, as Longinus' text proceeds, something strange begins to happen. Wealth is at its most dangerous when its power is 'measureless'. The parity between this notion of wealth and the nature of the sublime is, however, merely formal. For, unlike the sublime, the grandeur of wealth is superficial and does not work to elevate the soul but rather to wither and ruin it. The implication of Longinus' observation is, therefore, that the true sublime is on the side of morality.

GOD AND THE SUBLIME

The men of 'service and utility ... for all their faults, tower far above mortal stature', and while other 'literary qualities prove their users to be human; sublimity raises us towards the spiritual greatness of god' (42). *On Sublimity* makes frequent references to concepts of deity. Plato is 'divine' (6). The orator Demosthenes has 'divine gifts' (41), and while 'accuracy' may be admired in art and nature, 'something higher than human is sought in literature' (43). Significantly, Longinus cites as one of the highest examples of the sublime chapter 1, verse 3 of the Book of Genesis: 'God said ... Let there be light' (*Holy Bible* 2001). As Richard Macksey argues, 'the pervasiveness of the author's metaphorics of light – in the manner of Philo [Alexandrian philosopher, 20 BCE–40 CE, who developed a synthesis of Greek and Hebrew wisdom]' – suggests that Longinus may have been a Hellenized Jew (1997: 2; see Longinus 1964: xxix–xxx). Hebraic concepts of the sublime would have been familiar to Longinus from Scripture dating from the same period as the *Iliad*. Psalm 139, for example, mentioned earlier, presents a God too 'high' (the Hebrew word is *sagab*) for human comprehension. In Isaiah verse 55, line 9, the Lord announces that 'as the heavens are higher than the earth, so are my ways higher than your ways, and my thoughts than your thoughts' and in 1 Kings 8, line 27, Solomon, the builder of a temple, proclaims 'heaven and the highest heaven cannot contain thee; how much less this house which I have built!'

The texts of the New Testament, composed around the same time as *On Sublimity*, present an entirely different rendering of *sagab*, the significance of which is crucial for our understanding of subsequent theorizations. The Gospel According to John (80–98 CE), for example, begins with an invocation of Genesis verse 3, line 1: 'In the beginning was the Word, and the Word was with God, and the Word was God.' Where John differs from Genesis, however, is in his understanding that the Word, under the new covenant, is both transcendent *and* material: 'And the Word became flesh and dwelt among us, full of grace and truth' (verse 1, line 14). Central to this new covenant is the idea of the Incarnation. According to Erich Auerbach, the 'humility of the Incarnation derives its full force from the contrast with Christ's divine nature: man and God, lowly and sublime, *humilis et sublimis*' (1965: 41). In the Christ story, the sublime is derived from the historical, linguistic, and material humiliation of the godhead. The Word, incarnated in flesh, enters human time and becomes words. Subsequent Christian commentators stress, however, that whilst the style of Scripture may be lowly, vulgar, and simplistic, the 'sublimity of the subject matter shines through the lowliness' (Auerbach 1965: 52). Here again we should note how the figure of light is used to displace the abject matter of the world.

The importance of *humilis et sublimis* to the Christian tradition is manifestly displayed in the writings of Aurelius Augustine (354–430 CE). A teacher of rhetoric in his younger years, Augustine went on, following a powerful conversion experience, to become Bishop of Hippo and an influential Christian theologian. In the following passage from the eighth book of *De Trinitate* (400–416 CE), Augustine gives dramatic focus to his struggle to conceive the ineffability of God:

> Behold if you can the soul, weighed down by the body of corruption and by many earthly thoughts of various kinds. And now behold if you can: God is truth. For it is written that God is light; not as the eye sees it, but as the heart sees it when you hear: 'He is truth.' Do not ask what truth is. For mists of corporeal images and clouds of phantasm will rise forthwith and confuse the clarity that flared up in you in a first impulse when I said: 'truth.' When the word truth is spoken, remain if you can in that first impulse which struck you as a flash of lightning. But you cannot; you fall back into this world of familiar, earthly things ... .
>
> (quoted in Auerbach 1965: 54–5)

Augustine's sense of the divine is rooted in the distinction, initiated by the Greek philosopher Plato (428–348 BCE), between physical and ideal objects. Objects of this world are, according to Plato, subject to time and change; the nature of such objects is therefore relational or comparative: a physical object may be pleasing or terrifying depending on the manner in which it is considered, the way in which it is represented. By contrast, an ideal object such as truth is timeless; its nature is fixed and is independent of discourse. Plato calls such ideal objects Forms or Ideas. The Form of truth is truthful in itself; it is the measure by which all earthly examples of truth must be judged (see Plato 1976: 197–213). Augustine accepts Plato's reasoning, but his direct, colloquial style transforms the rhetoric of abstraction into heartfelt personal drama. Using a combination of anaphora (the repetition of a word or phrase in successive clauses), *'Behold if you can ... Behold if you can'*, and antithesis (the contrasting of ideas using contiguous sentences or clauses), *'remain if you can ... But you cannot'*, the fall from the 'light' of God to the 'world of familiar, earthly things' becomes a matter of the heart, as well as of the mind. The struggle between the 'mists' and 'phantasms' of the figurative and the lightning flash of 'truth' has now entered the realm of the self. Though Augustine maintains that true sublimity comes from God, rather than from language, our commitment to the world of words ensures that our apprehension of this truth cannot be sustained.

For Auerbach, the marriage of the human and the divine, the humble and the sublime, reaches its apogee in the *Divine Comedy* by Dante Alighieri (1265–1321). Comprising three books describing a visionary journey from hell, through purgatory to paradise, the *Divine Comedy* is described by Auerbach as 'a sublime poetry on a level with the great models of antiquity' (1965: 232). To measure this claim it is helpful to compare the passage from the *Iliad* discussed earlier with the example Auerbach gives from the ninth canto of the *Inferno*, the first book of the *Divine Comedy*. In Auerbach's translation from the medieval Italian, the passage reads thus:

> And now there came, upon the turbid waves, a crash of fearful sound at which the shores both trembled; a sound as of wind, impetuous for the adverse heats, which smite the forest without and stay; shatters off the boughs, beats down, and sweeps away; dusty in front, it goes superb, and makes the wild beasts and the shepherds flee. He loosed my eyes, and said: 'Now turn thy nerve of vision in that ancient foam, there where the smoke is harshest.' As frogs, before their enemy the serpent, run all asunder through the water, till each squats at the bottom: I saw more than a thousand ruined spirits flee before one, who passed the Stygian ferry with soles unwet.
>
> (1965: 228–9)

The demons have blocked the path of Dante and have even tried to turn the poet to stone by confronting him with the Medusa's head. Dante's protector, Virgil, removes his hand from the poet's eyes so that he may see the 'one' from whom the souls of the damned flee. Like the Iliad, Dante employs a style in which rhetorical devices, though present, are barely perceptible. As Auerbach comments, 'there is nothing petty, erudite, or bombastic in this rhetoric; there is no exaggeration of the rhetorical that would destroy the effect of the sublime' (230). The poem departs from the Homeric model, however, in its treatment of the striding god. Where Homer nominates his god at the end of the first two lines, Dante delays this revelation, and even then does not state explicitly who the 'one' may be. But the distinction goes beyond mere style to embrace the theological. Dante scholars conjecture that the 'one' 'represents the figure of Christ and symbolizes Christ's descent into hell' (231). The divine, in other words, is once again humiliated by contact with the profane, only to be raised up again as a result of such contact. The humanizing of the sublime is given further emphasis when we consider the position of the poems' narrators. Homer is removed from his poem. He describes the passions of men and gods but the underlying tone is always the same: 'it is the tone of narrative neutrality, a kind of sublime serenity, equable, untroubled, almost playful, and by virtue of evenness and unbiased serenity, almost divinely sublime'. Dante, by contrast, is not only the narrator, he is also the suffering hero. Unlike the externalised sublime of the *Iliad*, the *Divine Comedy*'s sublime is internal; in echo of Augustine but in a manner that anticipates the Romantic sublime, examined in chapter 5, the poem describes events occurring within the psyche.

1 John chapter 4, verse 16 makes the connection between the human and the divine complete: 'God is love.' But love in this context is different from love as it is normally understood. The Ancient Greek text of the New Testament makes a clear distinction between *philia*, fondness, *eros*, sexual love, and *agape*, selfless or self-giving love. In this respect, Christianity departs from Platonism, which, for all its stress on the primacy of mind over matter, nevertheless associates judgements of beauty with the force of erotic desire. Despite the focus on the suffering body of Christ, the love of Christianity, and hence the aesthetics of the Christian sublime, seeks to overcome its origins in the flesh. Through *agape* the Christian sublime, one might say, is purged of *eros*, and just as the Father, out of love for humanity, sacrificed His only son, so the Christian loves selflessly and without reserve. Sublimity thus becomes

in this sense an act of self-abnegation, an impulse that springs from the soul rather than from the body. This is why, as Paul writes in his first letter to the Corinthians, love is 'greater' than knowledge. If now 'we see in a mirror dimly', then we will see 'face to face'; if now we 'know in part', then we 'shall know fully' just as we have been 'fully known' (chapter 13 *passim*); if now we glimpse at the lightning flash of truth, then we will abide with 'the Father of lights, with whom there is no variation or shadow due to change' (James chapter 1, verse 17). As Dante realises, at the close of the *Divine Comedy*, union with the Father comes only when the temporality of *eros*, manifested in the hero's love for the woman Beatrice, is displaced by the eternity of light (see Milbank 2004: 218–20).

GENDER AND EXCESS

In Auerbach's thesis, Dante's Christian sublime is presented as a logical progression from the heroic sublime of pagan antiquity. Whilst for obvious reasons Dante is not present within Longinus' treatise, the sense of a literary sublime emerging from the struggle between competing generations of poets certainly is. Love, in the Christian sense, has little place within such a scheme. As the critic Barbara Claire Freeman argues, Longinus' view of literary production is one in which 'Poets struggle amongst themselves to best one another' (1995: 17), entering 'the Lists, like ... youthful champion[s] ... ardently contending ... for "Glory and Renown"' (Longinus 1975: 37–8; see also Longinus 1965: 19).

Such a view is echoed in the work of the American literary theorist Harold Bloom. Most notably in *The Anxiety of Influence* (1973), Bloom contends that the prize of greatness belongs to he (and it is typically a 'he') who successfully bests his opponents in the struggle for literary priority. A late eighteenth-century poet, such as Wordsworth, thus attains the sublime by outperforming the example of his great precursor John Milton. The twentieth-century American poet Wallace Stevens gains his sublime when he, in turn, struggles with the influence of Wordsworth. To be sublime, in other words, the poet must wrest the potency of another poet. In continuation of this idea the critic Paul Fry observes that 'the Longinian sublime appears in a climate of antagonism, as rivalry between authors' (1987: 188). What Fry does not add, however, is the gendered nature of this rivalry. In Bloom's *Anxiety of Influence* female authors are notable by their absence; where women do appear, it is only as the negative foil to masculine ideas of power and performance, as a mode of excess to be encountered and overthrown. Grounded as it is in Freud's theory of the Oedipus complex, the Bloomian theory of influence seems unable to imagine the sublime except as violent struggle between authoritarian fathers and rebellious sons.

As an example of how femininity is treated in theories of the sublime we may usefully return to *On Sublimity*. The notable exception to Longinus' pantheon of male writers is the Greek poet Sappho of Lesbos (early sixth century BCE). Sappho's lyric 'phainetai moi' is cited as an example of how certain writers 'consistently select the most important … inherent features [of a work] and learn to organize them as a single body' so as to produce sublimity (Longinus 1965: 14; translation slightly modified). Russell reproduces a modern translation of this lyric by D. L. Page:

> To me he seems a peer of the gods, the man who sits facing you
> and hears your sweet voice
> And lovely laughter; it flutters my heart in my breast.
> When I see you only for a moment, I cannot speak;
> My tongue is broken, a subtle fire runs under my skin; my eyes
> cannot see, my ears hum;
> Cold sweat pours off me; shivering grips me all over; I am paler
> than grass; I seem near to dying;
> But all must be endured …
>
> (Longinus 1965: 15)

'Do you not admire', Longinus comments, 'the way in which she brings everything together – mind and body, hearing and tongue, eyes and skin? She seems to have lost them all, and to be looking for them as though they were external to her. She is cold and hot, mad and sane, frightened and near death, all by turns' (1965: 15). Longinus' emphasis on bodily 'unity', on Sappho's ability to bring disparate elements 'together' (1965: 14–15), despite his manifest fascination with the disintegration of that body (see Hertz 1985: 5), is cited by Freeman as a 'paradigmatic response to the irruption of a threatening and potentially uncontainable version of the sublime, one that appears to represent excess but does so only the better to keep it within bounds' (1997: 15). And just as Longinus presented a markedly altered version of the *Iliad* to support his thesis on Homer, so here Sappho is misread in order to support a certain reading of the sublime. As Freeman goes on to state: '[The poem] juxtaposes such apparent dualisms as life and death, hot and cold, or sanity and madness, not as Longinus would have it, in order to create harmony, but rather to unsettle the notion of organic form upon which his notion of the sublime depends' (19).

Longinus' stress on the mastery of excess contrasts, then, with Sappho's openness to 'self-shattering'. In Freeman's view, where the male theorist ultimately wards off fragmentation, the female poet 'insists upon it', for 'what is particularly striking about the poem ... is Sappho's affirmation of the need for 'the unlimited in which to lose herself'' (19). Love, for Sappho, in other words, is sublime precisely because it involves the lovers in a merging of identities, rather than a separation. Unlike the anxiety of influence, there is no attempt to conceive of the sublime as a struggle for mastery or possession. Like Dante at the close of the *Divine Comedy*, Sappho is more concerned with giving way to loss, albeit in this case a loss infused with echoes of a more carnal nature. When, at the end of the poem, the speaker announces she is 'near to dying', she describes a form of ecstasy, or transport, more radical than that envisaged by Longinus.

Just as the Christian reading of sublimity challenges the Longinian stress on seduction and domination, so feminism enables us to challenge the connection between sublimity and unity. For Neil Hertz, however, in a suggestive reading of *Peri Hupsos*, sublimity is brought about at exactly the moment when a text is brought into conflict with itself. In the Sappho example the emphasis falls neither on unity or fragmentation, on the assembling of the body or its dispersal in death, but on the tension between the two. The sublime, in other words, is a result of the co-implication of seemingly natural opposites: life and death, unity and fragmentation, God and man. Thus, in 'phainetai moi', the energy of love that destroys the body of the poem is transferred to the constitutive labour of the poet: 'For it is not simply a poem of passion and self-division but one which dramatizes ... the shift from Sappho-as-victimized-body to Sappho-as-poetic-force. As such it serves as a figure for both a certain disjunction and a certain continuity' (Hertz 1985: 7). Death becomes a structural element in the verse, a heady dose of negativity on which the divine afterlife of the poet is raised.

CONCLUSIONS

With Longinus' *On Sublimity* key questions are raised about the ontological and ethical status of the sublime. Does the sublime support or undermine the integrity of the self? Is the sublime subject to legal, ethical, and pedagogical restraints? If the ultimate example of the sublime is the omnipotence, omnipresence, and omniscience of God, how is this to be represented? Central to Longinus' text is the suggestion that the sublime occurs within representation whilst nevertheless annulling the possibility of representation (Milbank 2004: 212). Should the sublimity of God be considered therefore as a mere structural effect of the sublimity of language? We will consider this question in due course. On the issue of Longinus' fascination with gender, language, and excess, Neil Hertz and Barbara Claire Freeman represent two contrasting approaches. In Freeman's case, the Longinian emphasis on the Sapphic embrace of death appears to push *ekstasis* beyond the bounds of masculine reason. On this reading, sublimity is no longer subject to a desire for mastery and control, or, we might add, to Hertz's desire to describe the sublime as a 'pure' instance of figuration, disassociated from the body. As we have seen, however, the discourse of sublimity is invested in the effacement of its dependence on mere words, and in this respect the eroticisation of the Sapphic body could be construed as the ultimate textual lure. We will return to consider the implications of this investment in the following chapter, which looks in detail at Longinus' influence on British criticism in the late seventeenth and eighteenth centuries.

2

SUBLIMITY IN THE
EIGHTEENTH CENTURY

RHETORIC AND REVELATION

Longinus' treatise came to the attention of a select number of English readers in the late seventeenth century via the influential French translation and commentary of Despréaux Boileau (see Brody 1958). Although the Latin text had been available since 1554, and was translated into English as early as 1652 (see Monk 1935; rpt 1960: 20), it was not until the mid-1740s, following the widespread success of William Smith's 1739 edition (reprinted in Longinus 1975), that the concept of the sublime reached a wider public. In this chapter we will see how Longinus is taken up in British writing of the early eighteenth century. We will look, in particular, at the work of five influential theorists: Thomas Burnet, John Dennis, Joseph Addison, Anthony Ashley Cooper, third Earl of Shaftesbury, and John Baillie.

Before we proceed to assess the nature and extent of Longinus' influence on English audiences, however, we should consider the precautionary remarks of the American critic Marjorie Hope Nicolson:

> When the critics who have considered the problem distinguish between two 'Sublimes', they give priority, chronologically and qualitatively, to a rhetorical Sublime [the Longinian sublime]. ... If they consider the natural Sublime (the Sublime in external Nature), they

tend to classify it as 'a degraded form of Longinianism,' following upon the rhetorical theory, but debasing it, 'showing itself in an excessive emotion for natural objects in the external world'.

(1959: 29–30)

A critical distinction lies at the heart of Hope Nicolson's thesis. Where the 'rhetorical Sublime' focuses on the grand or elevated as an aspect of language, the 'natural Sublime' regards sublimity as a quality inherent in the external world. Theorists of the natural sublime, in other words, are engaged on a quest for the origins of the sublime. Rhetorical theory, however, is not averse to such speculation. According to Longinus, although rhetoric is the primary determinate of the sublime, it is nature that seeds the idea of greatness in man, and that inclines us to admire the grandeur of the Nile, the Rhine, or still more the ocean (1965: 42).

When Longinus is taken up in the Christian tradition, attention shifts from nature to the divine. Mountains, for example, are sublime because their grandeur manifests the glory of God. But whether the origins of sublimity are located in the external world or in the divine, the desire for origins is in itself significant. Why does the discourse of sublimity encourage this desire? Central to Longinus' treatise is a concern with the concealment of language. For the sublime to arise, and for it to be sustained, speech must appear natural and unmotivated; the sublime must hide its slavish dependence on words. Longinus' recourse to nature is an attempt therefore to ascribe an extra-linguistic origin to the sublime. As I suggested in the previous chapter, early Christian writers make similar claims for the sublime: a worldly figure, yet conveying a sense of divine truth, beyond the veil of words.

BURNET: *SACRED THEORY*

The desire to efface the material nature of human experience, in particular its dependence on the stuff of language, is thus key to our understanding of the sublime. To understand this point let us look first of all at an example of the so-called natural sublime, Thomas Burnet's *The Sacred Theory of the Earth*. Originally composed in Latin between 1680 and 1689 and then translated into English in a much-expanded version from 1684 to 1689, the interest of the *Sacred Theory* comes from its daring revision of conventional seventeenth-century attitudes to nature, as conveyed in these lines from the poet Andrew Marvell:

> Here learn ye Mountains more unjust,
> Which to abrupter greatness thrust,
> That do with your hook-shouldered height
> The Earth deform and Heaven fright,
> For whose excrescence ill design'd,
> Nature must a new Center find,
> Learn here those humble steps to tread,
> Which to securer Glory lead.
> ('Upon the Hill and Grove at Bill-borow', lines 9–16;
> Marvell 1952)

Mountains, in Marvell's vision are 'unjust', 'hook-shouldered' excrescences, which threaten to 'deform' the balance of the earth. As Hope Nicolson comments, there is nothing unusual about this vision. Seventeenth-century nature poetry celebrated the serene, charming, and lovely rather than the majestic, wild, and irregular (1959: 37). A smooth, well-ordered garden, offering ease and delight to the spectator, was preferable to the brooding intensity of the mountain crag.

When Burnet looks at the grand in nature, however, he records a markedly different response:

> The greatest Objects of Nature are, methinks, the most pleasing to behold; and next to the Great Concave of the Heavens, and those boundless Regions where the Stars inhabit, there is nothing that I look upon with more Pleasure than the wide Sea and the Mountains of the Earth. There is something august and stately in the Air of these things, that inspires the Mind with great Thoughts and Passions; we do naturally, upon such Occasions, think of God and his Greatness: And whatsoever hath but the Shadow and Appearance of the INFINITE, as all Things have that are too big for our Comprehension, they fill and overbear the Mind with their Excess, and cast it into a pleasing kind of Stupor and Admiration.
> (*Sacred Theory*, 1776 edition; quoted in Hope Nicolson 1959: 214)

The vast night sky and the majestic mountain peaks suggested to Burnet an image of infinity: 'they fill and overbear the Mind with their Excess'. Yet for all his enthusiasm, Burnet was at a loss to comprehend his response. The mountains, though undoubtedly impressive, were 'shapeless', 'ill-figur'd', and 'confused' (*Sacred Theory* quoted in Hope Nicolson: 210). How could he look upon such wild irregularity and maintain the sense of nature as the work of God (212)? Burnet and his contemporaries, after all, conceived nature as a work of beauty, founded on principles of order, proportion, and restraint. The vast irregularity of mountain scenery offended this belief, yet it was the mountains that conveyed an image of the divine.

In a distinction that we will see repeated throughout this book, a reasoned commitment to beauty thus conflicts with an emotional drive to sublimity. Though the conceptual distinction between the sublime and the beautiful awaits the publication of Burke's *Enquiry* (see chapter 3), the idea of the sublime as a mode of divine excess, disclosed only at the point where the orders of beauty collapse, is already in place. Thus order vies with chaos, the regular with the irregular, the small with the vast, and the rational with the imaginative. It is no small irony that the struggle to reconcile these conflicts leads Burnet to increasing flights of rhetorical sublimity. The rhapsodic cadences of Burnet's style, generated by the doubling of noun formations and the multiplication of connectives ('and ... and'), are thus themselves an instance of the sublime.

DENNIS: ORDER AND ENTHUSIASM

This quality was recognised by a number of Burnet's readers, including the influential literary critic John Dennis (1657–1734). Like Burnet, Dennis was moved to express his delight in the 'extravagancies' of nature 'in a language of extravagance and hyperbole' (Hope Nicolson 1959: 279). And like Burnet, Dennis struggled to reconcile his aesthetic preference for the order and regularity of beauty with his newfound enthusiasm for the sublime. 'Nature', he writes in *The Advancement and Reformation of Poetry* (1701), 'is nothing but that Rule and Order and Harmony, which we find in the visible Creation. The Universe owes its admirable Beauty to the Proportion, Situation, and Dependence of Parts. ... And nothing that is Irregular ... ever was, or ever can be either Natural or Reasonable' (quoted in Hope Nicolson 1959: 280). As a child of the Enlightenment,

Dennis regarded nature as a rational system. Yet his enthusiasm for the vast and irregular militated against this regard. Thus, whilst the 'prospect of Hills or Valleys, or flowry Meads, and murmuring Streams' produced 'a delight ... consistent with Reason', it was the 'Extravagancies' of nature that provided an intimation of the divine (278).

What the natural sublime represented to Dennis was a manifestation of the vastness, the power, and the terror of God. Yet nature itself could not be perceived as sublime without the operation of mental processes. 'Take the Cause and the effects together', he writes, 'and you have the Sublime' (quoted in Hope Nicolson 1959: 281). The sublime feeling of 'delightful Horrour' and 'terrible Joy' was brought about therefore by the interaction of mind and object (279). The cause of sublimity could not be located solely in one or the other.

In *The Grounds of Criticism* (1704), Dennis provides a more rigorous account of this relationship. The text begins with an invocation of the Longinian notion of poetry as elevated or rapturous speech, a language distinguished from prose 'because it is more passionate and sensual'. Dennis then goes on to distinguish between two kinds of passion: 'I call that ordinary passion, whose cause is clearly comprehended by him who feels it, whether it be admiration, terror or joy; and I call the very same passions enthusiasms, when their cause is not clearly comprehended by him who feels them' (Ashfield and de Bolla 1996: 33). An ordinary or 'vulgar' passion 'is that which is moved by the objects themselves, or by the ideas in the ordinary course of life; I mean that common society which we find in the world'. Dennis gives the examples of 'anger moved by an affront that is offered us in our presence' and 'admiration or wonder' aroused by the sight of 'a strange object'. Enthusiasm, by contrast, is a passion that is moved by the 'contemplation' of ideas or 'the meditation of things that belong not to common life' (35). As an example he presents his reader with the image of the sun as it occurs in meditation. Where in ordinary experience the viewer perceives 'a round flat shining body, of about two foot diameter', in meditation the sun takes shape as 'the idea of a vast and glorious body ... at the top of all visible creation, and the brightest material image of the divinity' (35–6). The idea, which, for Dennis, compels a feeling of 'admiration' (36), transforms the material object, suffusing its mundane status with iconic significance. Here, then, we have an instance of mind working on nature to create a feeling of the sublime. But it is that which exceeds nature that affords the maximum opportunity for sublime feeling. Greater than nature, more powerful than mind, and ultimately inexpressible, the idea of God trumps all. It follows that the greatest literary accomplishment will be poetry that attempts to convey such an idea. A poetry that gestures towards the unspeakableness of God, which works by 'ravishing and transporting' the reader, and that produces a certain 'admiration' mingled with 'astonishment' and 'terror', is thus for Dennis the highest poetry of all.

The analogy between rhetorical elevation and Christian 'enthusiasm' is sustained in the work of Thomas Stackhouse, whose *Reflections on the Nature and Property of Languages* appeared in 1731. Like Dennis, Stackhouse avers that Longinus failed to determine the cause of the sublime. He then goes on to offer the following definition: 'The imitation of nature is the sublime of orators, the imitation of what is above nature the sublime of poets' (Ashfield and de Bolla 1996: 50). Orators, in other words, represent the sublime and wonderful aspects of nature, and their discourse ravishes on account of its ability to represent, in sonorous tones, the extraordinary things of this world. The Christian poet, by contrast, is motivated by a love of the divine. To illustrate his point Stackhouse returns to Longinus' citation of 'let there be light': 'by showing that his word was enough to make all things arise out of nothing', Moses grants us an intimation of God's omnipotence. The author of the Hebrew law is thus shown to be superior in perception to Homer, whose loftiness is restricted to the ability to represent the great in nature, a distinction that Longinus, for all his sagacity, fails to develop further.

The eighteenth-century recuperation of the 'Hebraic', as opposed to the 'classical', comes to a head with the publication of the Anglican Bishop Robert Lowth's influential *Lectures on the Sacred Poetry of the Hebrews* (1787). Here Lowth, according to the contemporary theologian John Milbank, construes the sublime as a dramatic expression of divine power that 'is not so much something represented in language as something which irrupts through language as an expressive event: a figurative expression which is also in itself sublime' (2004: 217). Just as, in Genesis, God performs the sublime through his invocation of the existence of light, so Lowth identifies the sacred poetry of the Hebrews with an act of creation rather than representation. In Hebrew poetry the sublime is not a representation of nature but rather the repetition of a primal oracular act.

MILTON: *PARADISE LOST*

The belief in the superiority of the Christian imagination over its pagan progenitor provides the eighteenth-century commentator with a buffer against the more unsettling implications of the classical sublime. Wedded as it is to evocations of natural terror, the classical imagination lacks the ability to comprehend the abstract and the ideal, qualities that raise mankind to the level of the divine. It is no accident therefore that the poet most frequently cited by British theorists in this period is John Milton (1608–74), whose epic *Paradise Lost* (1667) provides the classical period with its necessary Christian supplement.

For Milton the sublime is identified with the transformational power of language. Just as in Genesis the creation of day and night is initiated through the power of the WORD, so in *Paradise Lost* poetic speech has the power to make or unmake a world. We are like God, in other words, in so far as language enables us to create *ex nihilo*, to render out of nothing. As the opening lines make clear, Christian language has the power to raise poet and reader above the merely pagan:

> Of man's first disobedience, and the fruit
> Of that forbidden tree, whose mortal taste
> Brought death into the world, and all our woe,
> With loss of Eden, till one greater man
> Restore us, and regain the blissful seat,
> Sing Heavenly Muse, that on the secret top
> Of Oreb, or of Sinai, didst inspire
> That shepherd, who first taught the chosen seed,
> In the beginning how the heavens and earth
> Rose out of chaos: or if Sion hill
> Delight thee more, and Siloa's brook that flowed
> Fast by the oracle of God; I thence
> Invoke thy aid to my adventurous song,
> That with no middle flight intends to soar
> Above the Aonian mount, while it pursues
> Things unattempted yet in prose or rhyme.
>
> (Book 1, lines 1–16; Milton 1980)

Soaring above 'the Aonian Mount' or Helicon, the sacred mount of the Muses, Milton asserts a desire that is unprecedented, god-like even, but at no point does he seek to usurp the power of his maker. As the poet writes later on in Book 5, the word of the fallen is an echo of divine creativity, a point hammered home with unsettling irony in the presentation of Satan:

> He said, and as the sound of waters deep
> Hoarse murmur echoed to his words applause
> Through the infinite host ...
>   (Book 5, lines 872–4; Milton 1980)

While 'the infinite host' responds to the word of the fallen angel, their 'Hoarse murmur' is a debasement of the sound of worship, the 'voice of many waters', as presented in 'Revelations' (19. 6). Thus while language is shown by Milton to be the source of the sublime, we are left in no doubt that the aspirations of mere human utterance pale before the genuine sublime of the WORD.

Milton's significance to poets and critics of the long eighteenth century is exemplified in these lines from Andrew Marvell's dedicatory poem 'On Mr. Milton's Paradise Lost' (1674):

> That Majesty which through thy Work doth reign
> Draws the Devout, deterring the profane.
> And things divine thou treatst of in such state
> As them preserves, and Thee inviolate.
> At once delight and horrour on us seize,
> Thou singst with so much gravity and ease;
> And above humane flight does soar aloft,
> With Plume so strong, so equal, and so soft.
>   (lines 31–8; Marvell 1952)

In addition to the Longinian emphasis on rhetorical flight, a 'verse created like thy *Theme* sublime' (line 53), Marvell highlights a crucial link between 'delight' and 'horrour'. As we shall go on to see, the idea of the sublime as a form of painful pleasure is of central importance to the history of the subject. What goads Marvell to celebrate *Paradise Lost* in these terms is his sense of awe at the yoking of two apparently irreconcilable elements: the idea of the divine and the limitations of language. 'Where couldst thou Words of such a compass find?' pleads Marvell, 'Whence furnish such a vast expanse of Mind?' (lines 41–2). The poet's delighted horror is derived therefore from the residual antagonism between the sacred and the profane; an antagonism that points in turn to the vexed question of the origins of the sublime, a question to which we will now return.

ADDISON: ON DESCRIPTION

The endeavour to locate a source for the sublime, which most eighteenth-century thinkers believed Longinus had failed to achieve, is a pre-eminent concern in writings of the period. Typically, writers begin with a catalogue of those objects in nature most likely to inspire thoughts of wonder or astonishment. Joseph Addison (1672–1719), for example, in an essay taken from a series known collectively as 'The Pleasure of the Imagination', published in the *Spectator* magazine between 21 June and 3 July 1712, offers the following account:

> Such are the Prospects of an open Champian Country, a vast uncultivated Desart, of huge Heaps of Mountains, high Rocks and Precipices, or a wide Expanse of Waters, where we are not struck with the Novelty or Beauty of the Sight, but with that rude kind of Magnificence which appears in many of these stupendous Works of Nature. Our Imagination loves to be filled with an Object, or to graspe at any thing that is too big for its Capacity. We are flung into a pleasing Astonishment at such unbounded Views, and feel a delightful Stillness and Amazement in the Soul at the Apprehension of them.
> (from the *Spectator* 412, Monday, 23 June 1712; 1965: 540)

Not content with describing the effects of these sights on the imagination, Addison goes on to enquire into its origins. Like Burnet, Addison maintains that the underlying cause of greatness rests on the side of the naturally magnificent object. In a distinction derived from the empiricist philosopher John Locke (1632–1704), Addison insists that the 'Primary Pleasures of the Imagination' are stimulated by the

'Sight' of such objects, and that the 'Secondary Pleasures of the Imagination ... flow from the Ideas of visible Objects' (*Spectator* 411; 1965: 537). On the strength of this distinction, Marjorie Hope Nicolson argues that 'rhetorical ideas' were 'secondary' in Addison's scheme, and that 'they had a "great dependence" upon primary ideas coming to man direct from Nature' (1959: 310).

Our ideas of the sublime are thus rooted in sense perceptions; what we conceive is inspired by what we see. Still this does not explain why human beings should be driven to appreciate the 'greatness' of nature over its more beautiful aspects. Influenced, like Dennis, by the Neoplatonic idea of Nature-as-system, Addison regards 'a beautiful prospect' as an object of delight: 'We are struck, we know not how, with the Symmetry of any thing we see, and immediately know the Beauty of an Object, without enquiring into the particular Causes and Occasions of it' (*Spectator* 411; 1965: 538). Faced with beauty, the 'Soul' is content merely to 'delight' in what it conceives; it is 'greatness' that prompts the soul to investigate the 'particular causes' of delight (538).

This Addison attempts to pursue in *Spectator* 413. From the outset, however, it is made clear that since 'we know neither the Nature of an Idea, nor the Substance of a Human Soul', then it is impossible to 'trace out the several necessary and efficient Causes from whence the Pleasure or Displeasure arises' (1965: 548). The impetus by which an idea is produced cannot be established with any certainty; what Addison can be certain of, however, is why we should be so impelled. The ultimate cause is God:

> One of the Final Causes of our Delight in any thing that is great, may be this. The Supreme Author of our Being has so formed the Soul of Man, that nothing but himself can be its last, adequate, and proper Happiness. Because, therefore, a great Part of our Happiness must arise from the Contemplation of his Being, that he might give our Souls a just Relish of such a Contemplation, he has made them naturally delight in the Apprehension of what is Great or Unlimited.
>
> (543)

Man is created in God's image, therefore he is conditioned to delight in 'what is Great or Unlimited'. Just as 'Our Admiration ... immediately rises at the Consideration of any Object that takes up a great deal of room in the Fancy', a vast mountain range, for example, so the contemplation of God, who is the final consideration for us, will lead our minds 'into the highest pitch of Astonishment and Devotion' (543).

The Deity, Addison reasons, is 'neither circumscribed by Time nor Place'. He is moreover indescribable, not 'to be comprehended by the largest Capacity of a Created Being' (545). There are certain sublime phenomena, however, for example storms, earthquakes, and other disasters, that are subject to what Addison, in *Spectator* 416, calls 'Descriptions' (1965: 558). Indeed, Addison goes on to imply in 418 that their greatness is a consequence not of any inherent quality but of an act of reflection. For Addison, the nature of this particular mode of greatness 'does not arise from the Description of what is Terrible, as from the Reflection we make on our selves at the time of reading it' (1965: 568). Reflection can transform our perception of even the most 'hideous' of objects. As Addison continues:

> When we look on such hideous Objects, we are not a little pleased to think we are in no Danger of them. We consider them at the same time, as Dreadful and Harmless; so that the more frightful Appearance they make, the greater is the Pleasure we receive from the Sense of our own Safety. In short, we look upon the Terrors of a Description, with the same Curiosity and Satisfaction that we survey a dead Monster. … It is for the same Reason that we are delighted with the reflecting upon Dangers that are past, or in looking on a Precipice at a distance, which would fill us with a different kind of Horrour, if we saw it hanging over our Heads.
>
> (568)

In this passage Addison comes to recognise the importance of rhetoric or 'Description'. He also inadvertently suggests an alternative to his earlier naturalistic account of the sublime. Here, as Ashfield and de Bolla suggest, it is rhetoric that allows the mind to compare 'the ideas that arise from words, with the ideas that arise from the objects themselves' (1996: 67). Thus in the case of the 'hideous' object such as 'a Dung-hill' (*Spectator* 418; 1965: 567), the cause of pleasure resides in our capacity to understand and admire the transformational capacity of language; or,

to be more precise, to delight in the artistry that can change a threatening physical presence into a mental image that no longer 'presses too
closely upon our senses' (Ashfield and de Bolla 1996: 68). Art is
required, in other words, to convert physical threat into 'pleasing astonishment' (Hope Nicolson 1959: 306).

At this stage it is important to grasp that for Dennis, Addison, and
other early eighteenth-century theorists, the sublime emerges at the
point where the grand or terrifying object is converted into an idea. As
the critics Ashfield and de Bolla (1996) argue, the overwhelming proximity of the mountain, the earthquake, or the monster becomes ideal
and thus sublime as a result of the transformational power of language
or 'description'. Words allow us to make comparisons between things,
to make conceptions, to perceive objects as ideas and thus to regard the
threatening proximity of things from a position of safety. The natural
sublime, as conceived by Dennis and Addison, therefore offers ironic
testimony to the triumph of the rational over the real.

SHAFTESBURY: EMBRACING THE IDEAL

There are some objects, however, which are inherently sublime: the
greatness of God, for instance, is independent of mere description. Such
notions are rooted in Platonic notions of the distinction between real
and ideal objects, as advanced by the Alexandrian philosopher Plotinus
(c. 205–70 CE). Unlike real objects, which suffer the effects of time,
ideal objects, such as the soul, the concept of mind, and the good, are
immutable. Whilst the nature of real objects varies according to the
manner in which they are represented, the nature of the ideal object is
constant and is not dependent on mere description. This is why for
Addison the concept of heaven will always be sublime, irrespective of
the language or imagery that is used to describe it, and why a storm,
which is merely an aspect of the divine, is sublime only when it is
described as such. Unlike the sublimity of heaven, the sublimity of the
storm is relational, not inherent.

The Platonic displacement of the senses, the search for ideal objects
over and above the fallen objects of this world, is crucial to the development of the sublime. In the work of Anthony Ashley Cooper, third Earl
of Shaftesbury (1671–1713), much turns therefore on the classical dis-

tinction between objects in themselves and objects considered in relation to the world. As befits its subject, Shaftesbury's writing is notable for its 'enthusiasm' – a term which, through association with dissenting Christianity, had fallen into disrepute but which in itself 'signifies divine presence, and was made use of by [Plato] to express whatever was sublime in human passions' (from *The Moralists: A Philosophical Rhapsody*, 1709, quoted in Hope Nicolson 1959: 297–8). Here is a representative passage from the author's *Characteristicks of Men, Manners, Opinions, Times* (1711; this section first published in *The Moralists*):

> But behold! Through a vast tract of sky before us, the mighty Atlas rears his lofty head, covered with snow, above the clouds. Beneath the mountain's foot, the rocky country rises into hills, a proper basis of the ponderous mass above: where huge embodied rocks lie piled on one another, and seem to prop the high arc of heaven. See! With what trembling steps poor mankind treads the narrow brink of the deep precipices! From whence with giddy horror they look down, mistrusting even the ground which bears them; whilst they hear the hollow sounds of torrents underneath, and see the ruin of the impending rock; with falling trees which hang with their roots upwards, and seem to draw more ruin after them. Here thoughtless men, seized with the newness of such objects, become thoughtful, and willingly contemplate the incessant changes of this earth's surface.
>
> (Ashfield and de Bolla 1996: 76)

Notable for its fascination with the grandeur of Alpine scenery, a passion that would dominate the pre-Romantic imagination later in the century, the passage, with its bold declamatory style, its piling up of subordinate clauses with no organising centre, is a manifestation of the *Characteristicks'* principal theme: the endeavour to locate and maintain a position of 'rest' over and above 'the disorders of the corporeal world' (76). Though '*enthusiasm*' appeared to echo such disorder, its effects were analogous to the 'transports of poets, the sublime of orators [and] the rapture of musicians' (77). In each case, the aim is the same: the raising of the mind from its dependence on the sensual things of the world to a perception of underlying intellectual and moral harmony.

As Shaftesbury's prose sought to demonstrate the balancing of cosmic order and rhetorical *ekstasis*, so also it aimed to instil a sense of the ultimate goodness of the universe. Drawing again on Plato, Shaftesbury goes on to claim that the mind is in accord with itself and with the universe when it recognises that 'what is beautiful is harmonious and proportionable; what is harmonious and proportionable is true; and what is at once both beautiful and true is, of consequence, agreeable and good' (*Miscellaneous Reflections* III, 2, quoted in Fairer and Gerrard 1999: 316; see also Plato 1951: 95). It is important to note that here the sublime is not opposed to the beautiful, as it was for Dennis and to some extent for Addison, but rather works in concert with it to assist the mind in its ascent from corporeal distraction to visionary perception.

Welding Platonism on to eighteenth-century theories of sublimity is, however, no easy matter. For one thing, the notion that the sublime may be identified with the concept of beauty, which as a thing-in-itself is unvaried and eternal, rests uneasily with the vertiginous highs and lows, pleasures and pains, that the encounter with the sublime is apt to invoke. Wedded as he is to a rationalist outlook, the author of the *Characteristicks* is troubled by the idea that anything in nature might exceed the control of the mind: 'It is mind alone which forms. All that is void of mind is horrid: and matter formless is deformity itself ...' (79). Instances of the beautiful, for example, are discernible by virtue of their resemblance to an idea of beauty, which already exists within the mind. Sublimity, however, presents the mind with a peculiar challenge: how to remain in control in the face of the unbounded and the unknown. One answer, proposed by the Jewish-Hellenistic philosopher Philo Judaeus in the first century CE, is to locate the point of sublime rapture within the sobering confines of Stoicism, the philosophical doctrine advocating indifference to matters of the world. Thus, when that mind is carried 'beyond the confines of all substance discernible by sense, it comes to a point at which it reaches out after the intelligible world, and on descrying in that world sights of surpassing loveliness ... it is seized by a sober intoxication' (from *On the Creation*, quoted in Fairer and Gerrard 1999: 311). Guided by his neo-classical love of reason and proportion, Shaftesbury is similarly loath to countenance any notion of the sublime that would place the mind in jeopardy. It is for this reason that the *Characteristicks* supplements its Neoplatonic conception of the universe with aspects of Stoicism, finding in the classical ideal of manly calm and endurance in the face of extremity a means of braving the wilder excesses of the sublime.

AKENSIDE: DESCANTING THE SUBLIME

As a follower of Shaftesbury and Addison, the poet Mark Akenside (1721–70) offers a representative view of how the sublime came to be expressed in literature of the period. His *Pleasures of Imagination* (1744; Fairer and Gerrard 1999), a contemporary best-seller, regards nature as a stepping-stone to a heightened perception of the divine. As such it must be distinguished from loco-descriptive poems, like James Thomson's *Seasons* (1726–30), which take a more earthly view of the sublime. Though Thomson attempts to incorporate his descriptions within a wider philosophical context, the main emphasis of his poem is on detailed evocations of various natural phenomena. Thus, whilst Thomson paints storms, mountains, and desert landscapes as specific instances of terror and delight, Akenside, by contrast, looks to nature merely as 'a goodly frame' (line 1) in which to develop larger meditations on the relations between beauty, knowledge, truth, and goodness. *The Pleasures of Imagination* is thus concerned less with the sublime in nature and more with the sublime as a quality of mind.

First among the capacities that reside in the breast of the animated soul, be he a poet or a philosopher, is the ability to transcend the bounds of corporeality. Once freed of the 'mists of passion and of sense' (line 161), the animated soul looks down upon the things of this world, such as mountains, rivers, deserts, and empires, with Stoic disdain. Eager to embrace the 'Majestic forms' (line 171) of pure reason, the soul 'springs aloft

> Thro' fields of air; pursues the flying storm;
> Rides on the volley'd lightning thro' the heav'ns;
> Or yok'd with whirldwinds and the northern blast,
> Sweeps the long tract of day. Then high she soars
> The blue profound, and hovering o'er the sun
> Beholds him pouring the redundant stream
> Of light ... .
> (Fairer and Gerrard 1999: lines 187–93)

The realm of Platonic Forms is bathed in white radiance, a refulgent beauty that to mortal sight soon proves excessive. Overpowered by such vision, the soul plunges into the abyss, where it is 'swallow'd up / In that immense of being' (lines 208–9). Philo Judaeus's evocation of 'sober intoxication' is taken a step further here, so that divine communion is inseparable from the destruction of mortal bounds. True enough, it is the 'soul' or imagination that undertakes this step, but the fact remains that the evocation of sublime cognition is bound up with the rhetoric of annihilation. Thus whilst Akenside follows Shaftesbury in hymning the pre-eminence of the human mind – 'MIND, MIND alone bear witness, earth and heav'n! / The living fountains in itself contains / Of beauteous and sublime' (lines 481–3) – he also attests to the darker side of such elevation. The apotheosis of consciousness is unimaginable without some form of sacrifice. But whereas in Dante or Milton the extinction of the self is presented within the framework of *agape*, a pure, overwhelming love in the face of God, with Akenside the attestation of a presence beyond mind seems curiously constrained, even formal. This delicacy extends to the poem's treatment of good and evil. Although educated within the nonconformist Church, Akenside's religious sensibility lacks the agonistic qualities of the Miltonic imagination. Influenced, as we have noted, by the moral sense school with its emphasis on the Stoic acceptance of fate and the Neoplatonic equation of truth and beauty, book 3 of *The Pleasures of Imagination* suggests that irrational impulses or passions are not devoid of reason, but rather misappropriations of it. Hence notions of death, transgression, and fate, central to Burnet's and Dennis's sublime, whilst present in the poem are nevertheless drained of affect. The apotheosis of Akenside's poem is Horace's 'happy man', meditating on the 'charm / Of sacred order' and the 'elegance of love' (III, line 602 and line 605), untouched by the sublime irrationality of good and evil.

The enthusiasm for lofty ideas that motivates *The Pleasures of Imagination* is mirrored to some extent in the poem's style. Like many eighteenth-century poets, Akenside was a devotee of Milton and saw in the epic heights of *Paradise Lost* a mode of writing that was emotive and commanding and a sensibility that was raw and introspective, thus serving to qualify the predominant neo-classical aesthetic of poets such as Alexander Pope. Akenside may have been attracted to this aspect of

Milton's verse but, like his interest in the 'manly sternness and simplicity', the 'serene defiance' of the Stoic (Ashfield and de Bolla 1996: 85), the full scale of Milton's stylistic sublimity is reined in by the 'Augustan' virtues of elegance and refinement.

BAILLIE: DOING THINGS WITH WORDS

The order that Shaftesbury and Akenside perceive in the universe was undermined in the latter half of the eighteenth century by the spread of scientific materialism and philosophical scepticism. But, as Hertz and Ashfield and de Bolla have argued, the roots for an out-and-out decentring of the harmony between mind, beauty, virtue, and God were already implicit in the rhetorical concept of the sublime. For those writing after Longinus, in the discourse of the sublime, language works insidiously to transgress the boundaries between things, allowing properties to be transferred from one object to another, so that anything, even a dunghill, may be raised to a point of magnificence. The idea of Nature-as-system, central to Shaftesbury's Neoplatonic rendering of the sublime, for example, fades as notions of the transformational power of language begin to take hold. Once Longinian theory is taken to its logical conclusion, the notion that matter, informed by mind, possesses inherent meaning looks increasingly untenable.

The dramatist and essayist John Baillie takes up this point in his *An Essay on the Sublime* (1747). After beginning conventionally enough with the claim that a sublime 'Disposition of Mind' is 'created by grand Objects, the *Sublime in Nature*' (1953: 8), Baillie nevertheless admits that some 'Objects ... [that] are not great and immense, if long connected with such, will often produce an Exaltedness of Mind' (35). It is the notion of connection that should be stressed here, for what Baillie claims is crucial to our understanding of the discursive nature of the concept. In Shaftesbury's grand 'design', the relations between things are guaranteed by the presence of divine authority. God, the origin of this design, is thus responsible for animating the system, just as the writer is responsible for the 'order' of his text. By relating the disparate elements of the text, or the world, back to their origin in the consciousness of their author, relations in the world are perceived as being no longer arbitrary but natural.

Where Baillie departs from Shaftesbury is in his admission of the constructed nature of the sublime. '*Connection*', he writes,

> is a powerful Force. ... For by daily Experience we know, when certain *Pleasures* have been raised in the *Mind* by certain *Objects*, from an *Association* of this kind, the very same Objects themselves which first occasion'd them are not so much painted in the *Imagination*; and it is from this source that the Beauty and Delight of *Metaphor* flows.
>
> (35)

It is metaphor that enables us to transform objects into ideas. Just as the lover conceives beauty even in the 'Imperfections of his *Mistress*', in 'a *Cast* of the Eye, a *Lisp*, or any other little *Blemish*', so 'the gravest *Philosophers* also owe great Part of their *Pleasure* to this Stealing of *Beauty* from one Object to deck and adorn another' (34–5). Following this admission, Baillie is drawn to the reluctant conclusion that certain objects become sublime as a result of association, or connection. A building, for example, though falling short of that '*Largeness* as constitutes the *Sublime*', may yet raise ideas of riches, power, and grandeur (35–6) through the addition of architectural features, such as columns, arches, and vaulted ceilings. Together these features form a code, which works like a language, to evoke a feeling of sublimity.

Drawing on the arguments of the Swiss linguist Ferdinand de Saussure (1857–1913), for whom the relation between words and things is always arbitrary (see Culler 1986), we should note that the elements of a building acquire their meaning not as the result of some natural connection between feature and idea, with the column, for example, suggesting ideas of strength and durability (see Baillie 1953: 36), but only as elements within a system of differences and relations. Just as, within a traffic light system, the colour red signifies stop only because it is not green, and the colour green signifies go only because it is not red, so the column in the architectural system signifies strength only on account of its contrast with the surrounding emptiness. As a result of this contrast, attention is drawn to the massive force required to keep the building from collapsing. A column that is not incorporated within the structure of a building signifies something different. Nelson's Column, for example, in London's Trafalgar Square, points skyward, suggesting the moral, social, and spiritual elevation of its subject, Lord Nelson. Here again, however, the meaning of this column is not derived from any natural or intrinsic quality. Lord Nelson's nobility is rather a function of his difference from and relation with the surrounding public square.

To return to Baillie. If the sublimity of buildings may be traced back to the operations of an arbitrary code, then why should this logic not apply also to the sublimity of natural objects such as mountains? Though Baillie proposes that the 'vastness' of mind and nature are in some way interrelated (6–7), such a conclusion would have seemed absurd to an earlier generation for whom mountains signified only the deformed and the execrable. The association between the vast in nature and the vast in mind is itself therefore a product of a system of thought, linking such disparate authors as Burnet, Dennis, Addison, and Shaftesbury. What Baillie adds to this system is the idea that systematicity itself may work blindly, without origin or tendency, and perhaps even without an author, for once animated by the combinatory or associative power of language, a power undetermined by God, mind, or nature, a mouse as much as a mountain may become a source of the sublime. Sublimity therefore no longer resides in the object, or in the mind of the beholder, but in the discourse within which it is framed.

The point is taken further in the work of the dissenting minister, scientist, and teacher Joseph Priestley (1733–1804), for whom sublime qualities such as grandeur and awfulness are derived not from objects but rather from the ideas we 'annex' to objects. Hence, with a glance towards Baillie, the temple or senate-house has nothing innately grand about it; sublimity 'arises from the use to which it is appropriated' and the ideas that are associated with it (Ashfield and de Bolla 1996: 122). Although Priestley does not go so far as to suggest that ideas of justice and religion are arbitrary, his decoupling of object and affect in sublime discourse raises serious doubts about the veracity of Nature-as-system. If mental association alone is responsible for the order of things, it becomes very hard to defend the concept of an underlying design in the universe, let alone to infer the presence of a supreme being, a divine author responsible for the relations between things. For even if the world is a text, it is perhaps, as I have suggested, more fitting to draw an analogy with the decentred, random connectedness of the Internet than the fixed WORD of God.

There may be no order to the universe, but is this the result of a fail-ure of perception on our part? The late eighteenth-century critic Frances Reynolds (1729–1807) comes to such a conclusion. In her *Enquiry Concerning the Principles of Taste* (1785), Reynolds argues that the attempt to identify a cause for the sublime is self-defeating since the sublime is nothing less than the *'ne plus ultra* of human conception! The alpha and omega. The sentiment of sublimity sinks into the source of nature, and that of the source of nature mounts to the sentiment of sublimity, each point seeming to each the cause and effect; the origin and the end!' (Ashfield and de Bolla 1996: 126). Reynolds' analysis turns on the rhetorical trope of analogy, the equivalency or likeness of relations. Thus the vastness of the Alps is *analogous* to the grandeur of God, and, by the same token, the grandeur of God is *like* the Alps. But to the enquiring mind, words and objects, like graven images, necessarily fail as figures of the divine; only a mind that has comprehended the inadequacy of nature and language can 'discover' what Reynolds call 'the true sub-lime':

> It is a pinnacle of beatitude, bordering upon horror, deformity, mad-ness! An eminence from whence the mind, that dares to look farther is lost! It seems to stand, or rather to waver, between certainty and uncertainty, between security and destruction. It is the point of terror, of undetermined fear, of undetermined power!
>
> (126)

For Reynolds, true sublimity occurs at 'the point' where the distinctions between categories, such as cause and effect, word and thing, object and idea, begin to break down. The moment is religious because it also marks the limits of human conception, the point at which reason gives way to madness, certainty to uncertainty, and security to destruction.

CONCLUSIONS

We have journeyed some way from Longinus' original treatise. Yet for all the stylistic contortions and intellectual probing of his eighteenth-century followers, the basic elements of *On Sublimity* anticipate much of what is to follow. The problem of definition or lack thereof, for instance, becomes a central preoccupation of these theorists. Only Reynolds comes close to admitting that the quest for definition is self-defeating since the sublime is precisely that which frustrates the distinction between cause and effect. Similarly, in the field of rhetoric, most followers agree that there is no single figure or trope that will stand as a definitive example of the sublime. This leads Addison and Baillie to insist on the relational or comparative nature of sublime discourse: an object is sublime if it can be described as such. The problem with rhetorical indeterminacy, however, is when it blurs into questions of the ontological status of the sublime. Does the sublime have its cause in objects of nature or in ideas of the mind? The Platonic solution to this conundrum is to link the sublime with the timeless, ideal existence of the pure Idea. In a simple formula, matter does not matter unless it is informed by human capacities, the cognisance of beauty, truth, and virtue, which are a manifestation of the divine. Thus, for Christian and Neoplatonic thinkers of the period, the sublime, in its purest form, is emblematic of the creative power of God, that point of stillness beyond the veil of the contingent. It is when the sublime is considered as an aspect of language, however, that the concept is freed up from its slavish dependence on the natural world. For thinkers as varied as Dennis, Addison, Shaftesbury, Baillie, Priestley, Lowth, and Reynolds, what the sublime embodies is nothing less than the transformational power of language, its ability to link disparate entities (both physical and mental objects) by analogy. And what this power evokes, in turn, is of course the ontological status or lack of status of the human mind, a conclusion that evokes equal measures of terror and delight in the minds of Christians, Neoplatonists, and materialists alike; a conclusion, in short, that is quintessentially sublime.

3

BURKE

A PHILOSOPHICAL ENQUIRY

WORDS, THINGS, AND FEELINGS

In this chapter we will look closely at the work of the political philosopher, pamphleteer, and Whig Member of Parliament Edmund Burke, whose aesthetic treatise *A Philosophical Enquiry into the Origin of Our Ideas of the Sublime and Beautiful*, published anonymously in 1757, has had a massive and lasting impact on discussion of the sublime. That Burke's *Enquiry* far exceeded, in terms of scope and intellectual acuity, the outpourings of previous writers on this topic is manifest as soon as we consider the working relation to its closest competitor, John Baillie's *An Essay on the Sublime* (1747). As outlined in the previous chapter, in Baillie's work we reach the point where the contradictory nature of the sublime falls into crisis. Having determined that the sublime is a function of the combinatory power of language, and not merely a quality inherent in certain words and objects, or for that matter in the divine, the stress begins to fall on ways of accounting for this phenomenon.

The title of Burke's treatise, with its emphasis on the cognitive dimensions of the sublime ('Our Ideas'), gives a clue to this new trajectory. For Burke, the 'source of the sublime' is 'whatever is in any sort terrible, or is conversant about terrible objects, or operates in a manner analogous to terror' (Burke 1990: 36). The first part of this definition appears to confirm Burke as an advocate of the natural sublime, in the tradition of Burnet, Dennis, and Addison. Yet, as the sentence proceeds, the idea that sublimity is a quality inherent in certain objects begins to fade; the rhetoric of conversance and analogy shifts the origins of the sublime away from physical things and towards mental states. The trajectory does not end here, however, as, in a further development, we notice that the sentence itself has become obscure and inscrutable, a formal demonstration of the 'expressive uncertainty' (Ashfield and de Bolla 1996: 134) through which sublimity is conveyed. This seems to confirm that the origins of the sublime reside in words rather than ideas.

The ambiguity of Burke's brief definition of the sublime is typical of the *Enquiry* as a whole. For whilst at no point does Burke concede the radical possibility that sublimity is an effect of language, his argument seems constantly to be on the verge of declaring this possibility. This self-subversive tendency in Burke's text extends even to the apparent distrust of the natural sublime, for although sublimity appears to float free of corporeal origins, Burke insists that sense impressions are 'the great originals of all our ideas' (1990: 22). As a follower of the empiricist school of philosophy, Burke maintains that our knowledge of the world is derived entirely from the evidence of the senses: what we can see, taste, touch, and smell. The argument of the treatise, in contrast to that of his predecessors, is thus almost entirely secular; God is no longer required to guarantee the authenticity of our experience. Why, for example, the ocean should be a source of terror is explained as follows: in contemplating a large body, Burke conjectures, the eye is struck by 'a vast number of distinct points'. With its capacity stretched, so to speak, to the limit, the eye 'vibrating in all its parts must approach near to the nature of what causes pain, and consequently must produce an idea of the sublime' (124–5). There is no need to attribute this force to the power of the divine. The link between the exertion of the body and the mental strain of cognition thus brings a new psycho-physiological twist to Dennis's 'terrible Joy'. It is not that the dilation of the pupil is analogous to the expansion of the mind, but rather that it actually produces the idea of the sublime. By adopting the language of empiricism, Burke appears to recast the sublime as an object not only of philosophical but also of scientific enquiry.

Elsewhere, however, Burke seems less secure in this belief. It is one thing, for instance, to claim that my feeling of lethargy is caused by the physical state of hunger and quite another to state that my idea of

infinity is produced by eyestrain. Where Burke's empiricism clearly col-
lapses, however, is in his account of the relations between words and
feelings. As he writes in the section 'Of the difference between clearness
and obscurity with regard to the passions':

> It is one thing to make an idea clear, and another to make it affecting to
> the imagination. If I make a drawing of a palace, or a temple, or a land-
> scape, I present a very clear idea of those objects; but then ... my pic-
> ture can at most affect only as the palace, temple, or landscape would
> have affected in the reality. On the other hand, the most lively and spir-
> ited verbal description I can give, raises a very obscure and imperfect
> *idea* of such objects; but then it is in my power to raise a stronger *emo-*
> *tion* by the description than I could do by the best painting.
>
> (55)

In Burke's analysis, drawing and painting correspond to the empiricist
insistence on the intelligibility of the senses: a well-executed drawing of
a palace thus presents a 'clear idea' of its object. By contrast, even the
most exacting verbal description falls short of this requirement. Yet
although language fails to raise a clear idea of things in the world, it
succeeds as a means of 'conveying the *affections* of the mind from one to
another' (56). What words evoke, therefore, with greater force than any
other medium, is the entanglement of the objective and the emotional.

Now, as soon as emotions enter into the empirical calculus, ideas of
truth and knowledge are placed under considerable stress. For if the
authority of verbal descriptions is defined as purely affective, so that one
may persuade but not prove, evoke but not show, then it becomes very
difficult to establish the veracity of such descriptions. Yet as the *Enquiry*
points out, the expression of what 'really is' is not the concern of a theory of the sublime; where the 'former regards the understanding; the
latter belongs to the passions. The one describes a thing as it is; the
other describes it as it is felt' (159–60). Here again it is the affective
power of language that marks the limits of empirical proof and that provides compelling testimony to the mental terror that 'is a source of the
sublime' (36). 'To make any thing very terrible', Burke writes, 'obscurity
in general seems to be necessary' (54). It follows that whatever is
obscure, our ideas about death or the nature of existence, for example, is

terrifying and therefore sublime precisely because it cannot be presented to the mind in the form of a clear and distinct idea. As Burke argues towards the end of the treatise, 'there are many things of a very affecting nature, which can seldom occur in the reality, but the words which represent them often do'. Such words 'as war, death, famine, & c.', together with 'many ideas ... never ... at all presented to the senses of any men', but which 'have however a great influence over the passions', such as 'God, angels, devils, heaven and hell' (158), are properly described as sublime because they mark the limits of empirical understanding; one cannot, for example, properly experience heaven or hell, yet the ideas of such states exert a profound influence on our understanding of ourselves and of the world we inhabit. For this reason, 'Ignorance' is a crucial component of the sublime; 'Knowledge and acquaintance make the most striking causes affect but little. ... The ideas of eternity, and infinity, are among the most affecting we have, and yet perhaps there is nothing of which we really understand so little, as of infinity and eternity' (57).

To illustrate this point, Burke focuses his attention on the portrait of Satan in Milton's *Paradise Lost*:

> He above the rest
> In shape and gesture proudly eminent
> Stood like a tower; his form had yet not lost
> All her original brightness, nor appeared
> Less than archangel ruin'd, and th'excess
> Of glory obscured: as when the sun new ris'n
> Looks through the horizontal misty air
> Shorn of his beams; or from behind the moon
> In dim eclipse disastrous twilight sheds
> On half the nations; and with fear of change
> Perplexes monarchs.
>
> (Book 1, lines 589–99, as cited by Burke)

It is worth quoting Burke's reading of this passage at length:

> Here is a very noble picture; and in what does this poetical picture consist? in images of a tower, an archangel, the sun rising through

mists, or in an eclipse, the ruin of monarchs, and the revolution of
kingdoms. The mind is hurried out of itself, by a crowd of great and
confused images; which affect because they are crowded and confused. For separate them, and you lose much of the greatness, and
join them, and you infallibly lose the clearness. The images raised by
poetry are always of this obscure kind ... .

(57)

Writing of this kind 'effectually robs the mind of all its powers of acting
and reasoning', by virtue of darkness and confusion 'the mind is so filled
with its object, that it cannot entertain any other' (53) and is consequently 'hurried out of itself' (53, 57). Once again, in contemplating
that which exceeds the evidence of the senses, the self succumbs to the
combinatory power of language.

Later in his treatise, Burke offers a more precise account of this facility. With an echo of Baillie he reasons that 'by words we have it in our
power to make such *combinations* as we cannot possibly do otherwise. By
this power of combining we are able, by the addition of well-chosen circumstances, to give a new life and force to the simple object' (158). It is
language that enables us to select and combine ideas, so as to render
even the most unprepossessing object sublime, as another quotation
from *Paradise Lost* shows:

> – O'er many a dark and dreary vale
> They pass'd, and many a region dolorous;
> O'er many a frozen, many a fiery Alp;
> Rocks, caves, lakes, fens, bogs, dens and shades of death,
> A universe of death.
> (Book 2, lines 618–22, as cited by Burke)

Burke comments: 'Here is displayed the force of union in Rocks, caves,
lakes, fens, bogs, dens and shades; which yet would lose the greatest
part of their effect, if they were not the "Rocks, caves, lakes, fens, bogs,
dens and shades ... of Death".' To which he adds:

> This idea or this affection caused by a word, which nothing but a word
> could annex to the others, raises a very great degree of the sublime;

and this sublime is raised yet higher by what follows, a '*universe of Death.*' Here again are two ideas not presentable but by language; and an union of them great and amazing beyond conception; if they may properly be called ideas which present no distinct image to the mind ... .

(159)

In this startling passage, Burke argues that the sublimity of the phrase a 'universe of death' is brought into being by a power unique to language. The cloudiness, uncertainty, and terror of this idea is intimately linked with the combinatory power of language; it is words and words alone that allow the mind to link disparate entities together.

PLEASURE AND PAIN

In the previous section we saw how Burke's account of the sublime raises serious questions about the relations between mind and matter: is the sublime a quality that resides within objects of natural grandeur, does it have purely subjective origins, or is it produced in some way from the interaction of mind and object? Still more radically, is the sublime a mere effect of language? Burke's unwillingness to present decisive answers to these questions is prompted in part by his instinctive empiricism: a mode of thinking that restricts enquiry to that which can be verified by experience. Since a claim about the origins of the sublime cannot be proved, either by experiment or by reason, one must focus instead on its observable effects. The *Enquiry* is thus best described as a work of experimental psychology, a treatise that eschews the metaphysical in favour of patient delineations of the emotional states aroused by any particular experience of the sublime.

As mentioned earlier, Burke traces the source of the sublime to 'whatever is in any sort terrible, or is conversant about terrible objects, or operates in a manner analogous to terror' (36). The stress on the negative aspects of the sublime marks the crucial difference between Burke and his post-Longinian predecessors. Where Addison, for instance, regards the sublime as 'liberating and exhilarating, a kind of happy aggrandizement', Burke, by contrast, sees it as 'alienating and diminishing' (Paulson 1983: 69). A mode of pleasure may nevertheless be derived from this experience, as Burke continues: 'When danger or pain press too nearly, they are incapable of giving any delight, and are simply terrible; but at certain distances, and with certain modifications, they may be, and they are delightful' (36–7). The self may delight in sublime terror so long as actual danger is kept at bay.

Here Burke is indebted once again to John Baillie, whose 1747 treatise described sublimity as a 'contradictory' sensation of pleasure and pain: 'The Sublime dilates and elevates the Soul, Fear sinks and contracts it; yet both are felt upon viewing what is great and awful' (1953: 31–2). The key word here is 'viewing'. For Baillie there is a difference between engaging in a fight for survival and contemplating it from afar. Where the former involves a real possibility of annihilation, the latter treats it merely as an idea. To invoke a contemporary example: the experience of bungee jumping is pleasurable because the person who engages in this activity is reasonably certain that the elastic cord will rescue him or her from catastrophe. The bungee jump mimics the suicidal descent into the abyss, providing the person who falls with a glimpse of what that descent *might* really entail. Having exerted itself in this way, the individual feels correspondingly energised, more alive and thus more 'itself'. The impulse to sustain oneself in the face of danger is thus closely related to the experience of the sublime. To return to Burke's thesis, just as the eye contracts to preserve itself from the 'pain' of a blinding flash of light, so the 'I' shrinks into 'the minuteness of its own nature' in the encounter with terror (122–3). In both cases, 'self-preservation' (36), the passion for which resides at the heart of the sublime, is made dependent on a corresponding act of exertion: the eye and the 'I' are defined by their ability to 'labour' against destruction. If the self is lost in what Burke calls 'general society' (37), it is paradoxically recuperated in the 'painful' encounter with the sublime.

But the real question is whether such an encounter is moderated in all circumstances; are there not, as we discovered in the reading of Longinus, experiences that exceed the self-confirming labour of the Burkean sublime? To address this question let us consider the following passage from the section on 'Ambition':

> Now whatever either on good or upon bad grounds tends to raise a
> man in his own opinion, produces a sort of swelling and triumph that

is extremely grateful to the human mind; and this swelling is never more perceived, nor operates with more force, than when without danger we are conversant with terrible objects, the mind always claiming to itself some part of the dignity and importance of the things which it contemplates. Hence proceeds what Longinus has observed of that glorying and sense of inward greatness, that always fills the reader of such passages in poets and orators as are sublime; it is what every man must have felt in himself upon such occasions.

(46)

'Here', Peter de Bolla comments, 'Burke is describing ... the expansion of consciousness whereby the mind comes to an overwhelming experience of its own power' (1989: 71). The literary critic Steven Knapp confirms this reading, adding that 'the sublime itself now depends on an act of reference: the terrible object must be taken to signify a power in the self' (1985: 73). But as a power that is 'contemplated', and that is classed here, rather oddly, as belonging to the social, not the self-preservative passions (see Burke 1990: 36–8), the sublime of ambition appears to contradict the emphasis placed elsewhere on the external threat of pain and danger.

In this passage one might suggest that the sublime has been domesticated, raising ideas of 'dignity and importance' rather than fear and trembling. Moreover, as Knapp goes on to claim, there is an element of 'intellectualism' in this section, which runs counter to Burke's concern with physical immediacy as the 'efficient cause' of the sublime (see Burke 1990: 117–18). To put it more bluntly, the passage fails to convince because it is the essence of the sublime, surely, to resist mental appropriation. Recall that in the passage on astonishment, quoted earlier, the mind is so dominated by its apprehension of the sublime that 'its motions are suspended. ... Hence arises the great power of the sublime, that far from being produced by them, it anticipates our reasonings, and hurries us on by an irresistible force' (53). And again, in one of the few references to the divine, the mind is so 'struck with [God's] power' as to 'shrink into the minuteness of [its] own nature' (63). In each case, the enquiry into the source of the sublime, be it as a property of mind, of objects or of language, becomes a meditation on its harrowing effects, so that, in de Bolla's words, 'the full recognition of self-awareness, self-consciousness ...

amounts to nothing less than a desire for self annihilation' (1989: 70) –
this despite the qualifying emphasis on the maintenance of 'distance'
(Burke 1990: 36). Whichever way we look at the sublime of ambition,
whether it is considered as a social or self-preservative passion, the end is
the same: in both cases the self is led to the point of extinction.

ENGENDERING THE SUBLIME AND THE BEAUTIFUL

The fact that Burke's meditations are frequently couched in sexual terms
(sublimity is associated throughout with the imagery of tumescence;
beauty with the relaxed and enervated) lends an intriguingly sensuous
aspect to the treatment of self-preservation and society. If the passage on
ambition fails to convince the reader of the power of the sublime, could
this be related to the way in which the language of erotic excitement is
overlaid by suggestions of autoeroticism? The man who 'swells' in 'contemplation' of a 'power' that he has claimed for his own is protected not
only from the raw, unreflective immediacy of the sublime but also from
the self-destroying enthralments of erotic encounter. A few pages earlier,
Burke defines sexual 'generation' as decidedly social, 'of a lively character,
rapturous and violent, and confessedly the highest pleasure of sense' (37).
By contrast, the engorgement of self that takes place in the sublime of
ambition leads only to 'inward greatness' with no sense of blissful emis-
sion. The sexual expression of ambition reads like a bad parody of narcissistic regard, a non-relationship in which the self is insulated from pain
and danger as well as 'generation'. Yet here a further complication is
brought in, for while Burke is eager to define sexual love as a social pleasure, his emphasis on love's raptures draws his description perilously
close to the 'asocial (or even antisocial)' shores of the sublime (Ferguson
1992: 8). For although desire or lust is defined near the beginning of the
treatise as a social passion, in part three it is described as 'violent and
tempestuous', an 'energy of the mind, that hurries us on to the possession
of certain objects'. Here again, where love is linked with the 'contemplation' of beautiful 'things', lust is like the sublime in its disregard for
objects and in its resemblance to the excessive 'something', the nameless
'energy', which hurries the mind out of itself (Burke 1990: 83).

But this is not the only occasion on which love and desire run the
risk of upsetting the finer conceptual distinctions of Burke's argument.

One thing we have certainly failed to consider thus far is the founding opposition between the sublime and the beautiful. For Burke, beauty is 'a social quality': 'for when women and men ... give us a sense of joy and pleasure in beholding them ... they inspire us with sentiments of tenderness and affection towards their persons; we like to have them near us, and we enter willingly into a kind of relation with them' (39). There is, it is fair to say, a somewhat tepid tone to Burke's writing on the beautiful. Where the sublime 'dwells on large objects, and terrible' and is linked to the intense sensations of terror, pain, and awe, the focus of the beautiful, by contrast, is on 'small ones, and pleasing' and appeals mainly to the domestic affections, to love, tenderness, and pity. Crucially, with the sublime 'we submit to what we admire', whereas with the beautiful 'we love what submits to us' (103). The beautiful fails, moreover, as a support for ethical behaviour: 'the great virtues turn principally on dangers, punishments, and troubles, and are exercised rather in preventing the worst mischiefs, than in dispensing favours; and are therefore not lovely, though highly venerable. The subordinate turn on reliefs, gratifications, and indulgences; and therefore more lovely, though inferior in dignity' (100–1).

It should come as no surprise to learn that sublimity should be associated with 'the authority of a father', beauty with a 'mother's fondness and indulgence'. As Burke's Freudian biographer, Isaac Kramnick, observes, in the *Enquiry* 'sublime virtues are embodied in "the authority of a father", venerable, and distant. ... Mothers and women in general are creatures of "compassion," and the "amiable, social virtues" ... the masculine realm is [thus] authority associated with pain and terror; the feminine is affect – friendship and love associated with pleasure and compassion' (1977: 96–7)

For the cultural historian Ronald Paulson, similarly influenced by Freud, Burke's distinction between the masculine sublime and the feminine beautiful has more far-reaching consequences. Drawing authority from Freud's formulation of the Oedipus complex, Paulson cites a number of passages in Burke in which father and sons compete for the person of the mother. Focussing initially on Burke's allusion to Milton's portrayal of Satan (he who 'above the rest / In shape and gesture proudly eminent / Stood like a tower'), Paulson notes how the passage is preceded, two pages earlier, by the description of Death in book 2 of *Paradise Lost*:

> The other shape,
> If shape it might be called that shape had none
> Distinguishable, in member, joint, or limb;
> Or substance might be called that shadow seemed,
> For each seemed either; black he stood as night;
> Fierce as ten furies; terrible as hell;
> And shook a deadly dart. What seemed his head
> The likeness of a kingly crown had on.
>
> (Book 2, lines 666–73, as cited by Burke)

The deadly, or 'dreadful', dart (Burke is misquoting here) which Death wields is presented as a direct challenge to the assumed authority of Satan. As the 'king of terrors', Death is 'the ultimate sublime, the real father' (Paulson 1983: 68) striving to maintain dominion over the erring son. As Burke's text unfolds, however, his attention veers between the two figures 'so that we see him assuming the role of each challenger in turn', identifying, that is, with both the father and the son in their battle for priority (see *Paradise Lost*, Book 2, lines 681–725). Between these figures (though not identified by Burke) is the figure of Sin, 'the daughter-lover of Satan, the mother-lover of Death, suggesting a single powerful image of the son who challenges his father for the person of the mother'. As Paulson adds,

> The deep ambivalence of the emotion is patent in the fact that it is Satan, the arch rebel, who himself has become the father figure, and each insists on *his* being a king and father, the other a son and rebel. … It is first the feeling of the son as he challenges Death, and then of the 'son' Death facing his towering father Satan, as they confront each other, held apart by the mother-lover.
>
> (1983: 68–70)

Though the mother intervenes to calm the sublime wrath of the masculine principles, the pact between Satan and Death is established on the basis of their mutual detestation of God, the father of all.

Relegated to the role of peacemaker, the beautiful mother thus lacks the awe-inspiring qualities of the sublime father. According to Paulson, the mother is present in Burke's text merely as the object of masculine desire, a body to be fought over, appropriated, or merely elided, as in the Oedipal confrontation between God and Job, which follows the episode from Milton. In either case, the emphasis falls on the tempering of revolt, and the accommodation by which the rebel son comes to terms with the father, 'internalizing him as superego' so that he may himself become a father (Paulson 1983: 70). As was the case with Longinus, here Burke is concerned not only with the excess of the sublime but also with the conversion of that excess into a principle of internal discipline. To overcome the father, that is, the erring son must learn to become a father himself; the authority of the unfathomable must be symbolically appropriated. To draw this into the purview of Burke's treatise, the mind must recognise the sublime as a manifestation of its own power. In all this, the mother is reduced to a merely formal or procedural role. As an adjunct to the passionate contest between fathers and sons, she is little more than a passive device.

Burke, however, has more to say about the ambivalent role of the mother figure than Paulson is prepared to admit. Like Milton's depiction of the ambivalent Sin, half 'fair' woman, half hideous serpent, the feminine in Burke is defined not so much by her passivity as by her capacity for material excess. At first, the association of matter and femininity appears unproblematic. Noting that the 'cause' of beauty is 'some quality in bodies, acting mechanically upon the human mind by the intervention of the senses' (102; my emphasis), Burke maintains a conventional distinction between feminine matter (for which read *mater*, or mother) and masculine intellect. As an aspect of nature, the beautiful has little truck with the self-generating, dark, and obscure power of the masculine mind. Where the latter provokes awe and wonder, the former merely pleases; its power is merely conventional. Yet in practice the link between beauty and convention is not as benign as it might at first appear, for there is a sense in which repeated exposure to the sublime runs the risk of draining its intensity. As the taste for the sublime becomes fashionable, its ability to provoke awe or fear is diminished: after a while every mountain, even a Mont Blanc, fades into indifference.

Burke's insight into the vitiating effects of 'custom' (see Ferguson 1992: 46–7; also Furniss 1993: 69) recalls his earlier distinction between knowledge and ignorance: 'Knowledge and acquaintance make the most striking causes affect but little', and littleness, it should be noted, is yet another attribute of the beautiful. To become accustomed to the sublime is beneficial, then, in so far as the sublime is brought into the domain of universal assent ('it is agreed that Mont Blanc is sublime') and thus of society, but deadly since it results in the extinction of sublime singularity. Ultimately, the sublime is under threat, always on the brink of conversion into customary beauty.

Yet such is the indeterminate nature of Burke's distinction that beauty all too often presents a puzzling, even excessive, face to the eye of its beholder. 'Observe', Burke writes,

> that part of a beautiful woman where she is perhaps the most beautiful, about the neck and breasts; the smoothness; the softness; the easy and insensible swell; the variety of the surface, which is never for the smallest space the same; the deceitful maze, through which the unsteady eye slides giddily, without knowing where to fix, or whither it is carried.
>
> (105)

As justification of the idea that 'gradual variation' is an aspect of beauty, this description is puzzling, to say the least. The infinite variety of the flesh induces 'giddiness' in its masculine observer; like the description of the sublime, quoted earlier, the I/eye in this description is hurried along, unable to rest or to determine its destination. Ultimately, the infinite variety of the feminine form is said to be a 'deceitful maze', a judgement that rests uneasily with the pleasing and submissive aspects of the beautiful.

Matters come to a head when Burke addresses the so-called 'counterfeit' nature of the 'female sex':

> [Beauty] almost always carries with it an idea of weakness and imperfection. Women are very sensible of this; for which reason, they learn to lisp, to totter in their walk, to counterfeit weakness, and even sickness. In all this, they are guided by nature. Beauty in distress is much the most affecting beauty. Blushing has little less power; and modesty in general, which is a tacit allowance of imperfection, is itself considered as an amiable quality, and certainly heightens every other that is so.
>
> (100)

Like the sublime, the beautiful is invested with power, though of a deceitful and uncertain nature. Where, in one case, 'we are forced' to 'submit to what we admire', in the other 'we are flattered into compliance' (103). The sublime may well induce feelings of fear and trembling in its subjects, but unlike the beautiful it at least has the virtue of not pretending to be anything other than what it is. The more one examines Burke's thoughts on the links between femininity and beauty, masculinity and the sublime, the more troubling they become. For even as the opposition between masculinity falls into a hierarchical relationship, with man evidently at the top, Burke invests the scapegoat category of woman with powers sufficient to subvert its subordination. Indeed, the more one engages with Burke's text, the more apparent it becomes that the phallocentricism of his treatise is under constant threat from the excluded feminine other.

Nowhere is this more apparent than in the attention Burke gives to the vitiating effects of beauty. Writing on 'love', Burke notes how the body falls into a kind of stupor:

> the head reclines something on one side; the eyelids are more closed than usual ... the mouth is a little opened, and the breath drawn slowly, with now and then a low sigh: the whole body is composed, and the hands fall idly to the sides. All this is accompanied with an inward sense of melting and languor.
>
> (135)

Opposed, therefore, to the bracing tension of the sublime, and above all to its labour, is the relaxed mediocrity of love, a mode of the beautiful in which the rigours of identity become 'softened, relaxed, enervated, dissolved, melted away by pleasure' (136). Burke's masculinity is thus shown to be constantly at the mercy of feminine stupefaction. But Burke's anxiety in the face of beauty does not stop there. Writing on the political significance of beauty, he draws the following lesson from the portrayal of the Greeks and the Trojans in Homer's *Iliad*:

> It may be observed, that Homer has given the Trojans, whose fate he has designed to excite our compassion, infinitely more of the amiable social virtues than he has distributed among his Greeks. With regard

to the Trojans, the passion he chuses to raise is pity; pity is a passion founded on love; and these lesser, and if I may say, domestic virtues, are certainly the most amiable. But he has made the Greeks far their superiors in the politic and military virtues. The councils of Priam are weak; the arms of Hector comparatively feeble; his courage far below that of Achilles. Yet we love Priam more than Agememnon, and Hector more than his conqueror Achilles. Admiration is the passion which Homer would excite in favour of the Greeks, and he has done it by bestowing on them the virtues which have but little to do with love.

(143–4)

Pity may well be amiably extended to the defeated, but admiration is on the side of the victorious. The problem with love, as Burke implies, is that it tends to promote identification with the weak, where sublime admiration maintains the noble virtues of courage and distinction.

Frances Ferguson's commentary on this passage is especially apposite:

After the beautiful has been joined with physical and political entropy issuing in death, the importance of the sublime in exciting the passions of self-preservation becomes apparent. For although the sublime inspires us with fear of our death, the beautiful leads us towards death without our awareness … .

(52)

The sublime, moreover,

acts as the antidote to the dissolution produced by the beautiful. All its strainings follow the dictates of the work ethic: 'The best remedy for these evils (produced by the beautiful) is exercise or *labour*, and labour is a surmounting of difficulties, an exertion of the contracting power of the muscles …' [122].

(52)

Burke's text presents itself, therefore, as engaged in perpetual war with feminine lassitude. That society should be associated with the domestic or feminine virtues, and self-preservation with masculine principles of heroic exemption (the hero, like Cato, who goes against the code of everyday civic virtue in order to save his nation, is the apogee of the sublime), presents Burke with a fundamental problem, for it suggests that ordinary life is based on deceit:

> For while tyrants are sublime in the *Enquiry*, only the beautiful, with its commitment to companionable resemblance between humans, disguises the disequilibrium of power so effectively that we all, like Adam, become accomplices to our own deaths. Although the sublime masters us while we are superior to the power of the beautiful, the *Enquiry* suggests that we invariably misconstrue those power relationships by failing to recognize that what we term the weaker has greater sway over us than the sublime with its palpably awesome force.
>
> (Ferguson 1992: 53)

It seems therefore that Burke's privileging of the sublime is prompted by a number of fears: the lapse of the extraordinary into 'custom'; the collapse of masculinity in the face of feminine languor; and the fall of heroic identity into social mediocrity. For a book that invests so much in the awe-inspiring, implacable potency of the sublime it seems extraordinary that the real threat should come, not from the masculine realm of asocial (or even anti-social) self-aggrandisement, but from the feminine sphere of companionable dissolution. As Tom Furniss adds, 'Beauty's most pernicious quality of all, therefore, is that it gives the sublime nothing upon which to exercise itself or labour' (1993: 39).

REFLECTIONS ON THE REVOLUTION IN FRANCE

Some thirty years after the completion of the *Enquiry*, Burke extended the terms of his aesthetic analysis to the domain of politics. The event that prompted this renewed enquiry was the French Revolution, inaugurated by the fall of the Bastille in Paris on 14 July 1789. The idea that Burke's response to the Revolution, published in 1790 as *Reflections on the Revolution in France*, was profoundly influenced by his earlier aesthetic investigations is given credence by a passage from a letter, dated 9 August 1789:

As to us here our thoughts of every thing at home are suspended, by our astonishment at the wonderful Spectacle which is exhibited in a Neighbouring and rival Country – what Spectators, and what actors! England gazing with astonishment at a French struggle for Liberty and not knowing whether to blame or applaud! The thing indeed, though I thought I saw something like it in progress for several years, has still something in it paradoxical and Mysterious. The spirit is impossible not to admire; but the old Parisian ferocity has broken out in a shocking manner. ... What will be the Event it is hard I think still to say. To form a solid constitution requires Wisdom as well as spirit, and whether the French have wise heads among them, or if they possess such whether they have authority equal to their wisdom, is to be seen; In the mean time the progress of this whole affair is one of the most curious matters of Speculation that ever was exhibited.

(To Lord Charlemont, *Correspondence* 1967: 6, 10)

For Burke, the Revolution is an event of sublime theatricality. It is, first and foremost, 'a wonderful Spectacle', a 'paradoxical and Mysterious' art work 'exhibited' for 'Speculation', an enigmatic 'thing', which causes the minds of those who gaze upon it to be 'suspended' by 'astonishment'. To the man of taste, well versed in the discourse of painful pleasures, the French Revolution might indeed be regarded as a 'curious matter', even as an object to 'admire'. But the more one gazes on this object, the less the artistic analogies hold true. As Burke adds, 'the old Parisian ferocity has broken out in a shocking manner ... What will be the Event it is hard I think still to say.' The possibility that such ferocity might exceed its national boundary, infecting our safe English 'home' with the germ of insurrectionary violence, provides a disturbing counterpoint to the overarching attempt at contemplative detachment. It is perhaps not going too far to say that this passage marks the point at which Burke realises the political significance of his theory of the sublime.

The distinction between theatrical and actual displays of violence was a subject touched upon in the *Enquiry*: 'Chuse a day', Burke writes,

on which to represent the most sublime and affecting tragedy we have ... and when you have collected your audience, just at the moment when their minds are erect with expectation, let it be reported that a state criminal of high rank is on the point of being executed in the adjoining square; in a moment the emptiness of the theatre would demonstrate the comparative weakness of the imitative arts, and proclaim the triumph of the real sympathy.

(1990: 43)

Burke may insist here on the primacy of the real, and on its crucial difference from representation, yet both in the theatre and in 'the adjoining square', events unfold which engage an audience's 'sympathy'. The response elicited in the mind of the spectator is thus, in both cases, the same.

Between August 1789 and January 1790, Burke's concern with the vitiating effects of revolution was addressed in detail in the pages of the *Reflections*. 'It looks to me', Burke writes,

as if I were in a great crisis, not of the affairs of France alone, but of all Europe, perhaps of more than Europe. All circumstances taken together, the French revolution is the most astonishing thing that has hitherto happened in the world. The most wonderful things are brought about in many instances by means the most absurd and ridiculous; in the most ridiculous modes; and apparently, by the most contemptible instruments. Every thing seems out of nature in this strange chaos of levity and ferocity, and of all sorts of crimes jumbled together with all sorts of follies. In viewing this monstrous tragic-comic scene, the most opposite passions necessarily succeed, and sometimes mix with each other in the mind; alternate contempt and indignation; alternate laughter and tears; alternate scorn and horror.

(1969: 92–3)

The revolution is once again 'astonishing' and 'wonderful', only now it is brought about 'by means', 'modes' and 'instruments' that are 'the most absurd ... ridiculous ... [and] contemptible'. The status of 'astonishment', which in August 1789 signified the dependence of the author's mind on the sway of external events, is rendered subordinate in this passage to the sardonic linking of the sublime with the ridiculous. Burke's capacity for satire, in other words, elevates the 'I' above the 'crisis'; what the prose enacts is precisely a *reflection* on divided subjectivity, a reflection that, by virtue of its capacity for rhetorical containment, immunizes the authorial 'I' from revolutionary contamination.

The rhetorical distinction between the integrated, self-determining 'I' and the 'monstrous', jumbled 'mob' is deeply implicated with Burke's contribution to theories of class. As Tom Furniss (1990) and Terry Eagleton (1993) have argued, it is possible to see in both the *Enquiry* and the *Reflections* allegories for the emergence and persistence of modern bourgeois identity. Crucially, what the *Reflections* set out to achieve is a reclamation of the sublime, based on a distinction between the pernicious inflation of revolutionary discourse and the 'natural' hier-archies embedded in the British constitution. For Burke, 'the spirit of freedom, leading [in France] to misrule and excess is tempered [in Britain] by an awful gravity'. Where the French 'citizen' bases his enthusiasm on the false glare of revolutionary zeal, indissoluble ties to ancient and noble traditions bind the British 'subject'. As Burke con-cludes,

> This idea of a liberal descent inspires us with a sense of habitual native dignity, which prevents that upstart insolence almost inevitably adhering to and disgracing those who are the first acquirers of any distinction. By this means our liberty becomes a noble freedom. It carries an imposing and majestic aspect.
>
> (1969: 121)

The British constitution is sublime, in other words, because it main-tains 'awe, reverence, and respect' in its subjects. The French system is pernicious because it encourages a 'multitude' to revolutionary excess.

For evidence of the derisory effects of French enthusiasm on the stately and 'domestic' frame of British polity, Burke focuses on the con-cluding words of Richard Price's *Discourse on the Love of Our Country*, a radical pamphlet issued in November 1789. To instil enthusiasm in his listeners, Price adopts a familiar trope: the image of freedom as revela-tory light: 'Behold, the light you have struck out, after setting AMERICA free, reflected to FRANCE, and there kindled into a blaze that lays despotism in ashes, and warms and illuminates EUROPE!' In Price's writing, as Furniss comments, 'Light becomes a liberating sublime, driving out the false, oppressive sublime of darkness and obscurity through which kings terrorize the people' (1993: 118). Some thirty years earlier, in the *Philosophical Enquiry*, Burke had argued that 'darkness is more productive of sublime ideas than light', though he adds the qualification that 'such a light as that of the sun, immediately exerted on the eye, as it overpowers the sense, is a very great idea. ... Extreme light, by overcoming the organs of sight, obliterates all objects, so as in its effects exactly to resemble darkness' (1990: 73–4). In formal terms, therefore, the notion of a radical light appears to be in accord with the Burkean sublime. Politically, however, Price's coruscating fire, which Burke in the *Reflections* disparagingly calls 'this new-conquering empire of light and reason!' (171), could not be more distinct. Accordingly, a distinction is forged in the *Reflections* between the artificial light of the Revolution, which dissolves all 'the sentiments which beautify and soften private society' (171), and the natural light of the sun, which enters 'into common life, like rays of light which pierce into a dense medium, [and] are by the laws of nature, refracted from their straight line' (152).

New to this description is the emphasis that Burke places not only on the dense complexity of nature over the pellucid abstractions of theory but also on the redemptive role of beauty. Beauty returns, in other words, within the body of the *Reflections*, as a counter-spirit to the sublime, which lends itself, as the passage from Price illustrates, all too easily to radical appropriation. Recent commentators have read in the *Reflections* a significant critical revision of the *Enquiry*'s privileging of the masculine sublime and its corresponding denigration of feminine beauty (see Kramnick 1977: 93, 151–7; Paulson 1983: 57–73). The passage which fosters this view is Burke's startling description of the Jacobin assault on Marie-Antoinette, the French queen, with whom Burke was acquainted:

> History will record, that on the morning of the 6th of October 1789, the king and queen of France, after a day of confusion, alarm, dismay, and slaughter, lay down, under the pledged security of public faith, to indulge nature in a few hours of respite, and troubled melancholy repose. ... A band of cruel ruffians and assassins, reeking with blood, rushed into the chamber of the queen, and pierced with an hundred

strokes of bayonets and poniards the bed, from whence this perse-
cuted woman had but just time to fly almost naked, and through ways
unknown to the murderers had escaped to seek refuge at the feet of a
king and husband, not secure of his own life for a moment.

(1969: 164)

Here we encounter the venerated mother of the *Enquiry*, the feminine
principle of 'compassion' and social 'virtue', assaulted by the unbridled
masculinity of revolution. Significantly, though erroneously, the queen
is presented 'almost naked'. The imagery of nakedness, as Ronald
Paulson comments, prefigures the later passage in which Burke
describes the vitiating effects of 'this new conquering empire of light
and reason'. Under this new system, the stripping of the queen and the
stripping of society become the same thing (1983: 61):

But now all is to be changed. All the pleasing illusions, which made
power gentle, and obedience liberal, which harmonized the different shades of life, and which, by a bland assimilation, incorporated
into politics the sentiments which beautify and soften private society, are to be dissolved. ... All the decent drapery of life is to be
rudely torn off.

(1969: 171)

The tension in the *Enquiry* between illusory social concord and authentic sublime discord is touched on again in this passage. What Burke
finds appalling in the attack on the queen is that the unfettered energy
of the masculine sublime should be allowed to destroy the 'pleasing
illusions' which sustain everyday life. The image of beauty under stress,
the queen's bed 'pierced with an hundred strokes of bayonets and
poniards', is used by Burke to prevent his readers deriving delight from
the 'terror' of the Revolution, from seeing it as in any way sublime. In
this Oedipal version of events, the assault is presented as a challenge to
the rightful claim of the king, the father, to possession of the mother.
By symbolically appropriating the king's property, the mob also succeeds in internalising his power. And the result, for Burke, is truly hor-
rifying: a return to tyranny as the rebel sons, unconstrained by natural
law, battle for supremacy.

The idea of beauty, therefore, is used as a strategic counter to assist Burke's readers to make the crucial distinction between the false, or revolutionary, sublime and its true, constitutional, counterpart. Under the British system, Burke insists, the illusory comforts of domestic peace and social harmony are respected and sustained. When, however, revolution is allowed to hold sway over the minds of men, 'grown torpid with the lazy enjoyment of ... security', the sublime becomes a 'stage effect', sustained by outbursts of 'exultation and rapture' (1990: 93, 156–7). The pleasing illusions of beauty, which conceal the order of society, are exposed, and so we perceive 'the defects of our naked shivering nature' (171). Yet just as the *Enquiry* displayed ambivalence over the status of beauty and the feminine, so the *Reflections*, in that disparaging reference to the enervating effects of 'security', seems to query the privileging of the maternal. If a prolonged period of domestic security induces torpor, then surely it is 'natural' to expect some form of violent revolt – unless that is, the sublime is recognised as a principle internal to the constitution of the self and thus, by extension, to the idea of society. What the mature society perceives, in other words, is the dialectical relation between the sublime and the beautiful. And it is this level of perception that, for Burke, is an indicator of the true sublime.

And yet, as Tom Furniss has argued, the distinction between the true and the false sublime remains a problem for Burke. It is, moreover, a problem that is 'precisely inherent within the discourse of the sublime' (1993: 134). For if we go back to one of Burke's original ideas, namely that the sublime turns on the distinction between the raw immediacy of terror and its more pleasurable representation, then we can begin to see how Burke's attempts to distinguish between the false revolutionary and the true constitutional sublime run the risk of collapsing this distinction.

Consider Burke's dilemma. On the one hand he must portray the Revolution as ridiculous so as to maintain 'a certain ironic distance', Yet, at the same time, he must persuade his readers that the Revolution is 'sheer terror because it will not keep its "distance" '. In both cases there is nothing sublime about the Revolution. But since the proper reaction to terror is self-preservation, which involves the re-activation of distance and thus of reflection, Burke cannot prevent his text from generating what Furniss calls 'sublime reading effects' (1993: 135). The terror might well become a source of delight for the simple reason that it has become, in Burke's pages, an object of contemplation rather than an immediate danger. It is for this reason that Burke's imagining of the violation of Marie-Antoinette seems, on reflection, to veer precariously between objection and fascination, to become, in short, an object of the sublime.

As Furniss concludes:

> Burke's text seems caught up in an inescapable double-bind in which ecstasy and persuasion have contrary effects to those 'intended', each of which seems implicated within and makes urgent the other. The *Reflections* can therefore be read as if caught up in the same repetitive cycle it would attribute to the Revolution, alternating confusedly between terror and the sublime, delight and ridicule, each immediately compelling its opposite.
>
> (1993: 136–7)

Just as, in the *Enquiry*, the feminine principle of beauty threatened to exceed its allotted place, thus undermining the distinction on which the masculine sublime is raised, so in the *Reflections*, the separation of the 'radical' or false sublime from its 'authentic' counterpart becomes impossible to sustain. The integrity of the reflector is thus constantly undermined by its 'natural' tendency to elevate terror to the dignity of the sublime. It is, after all, what the mind craves, especially if, after thirty years of torpor, it is suddenly confronted by an inducement to labour. The danger, of course, is that its detractors should expose the outcome of such labour as a mere 'stage effect' with no foundation in fact or reason. For whatever the *Reflections* might have to say about the inherent sublimity of the British system, the fact remains that this claim would amount to nothing without the stimulus of Price's *Discourse*. Thus, as the radical Tom Paine suggests, through his subtle citation of Burke's rhetoric in the *Rights of Man* ('I consider Mr Burke's book in scarcely any other light than a dramatic performance ... a stage effect'; 1995: 110), within the discourse of the sublime there is no secure distinction to be made between true and false, natural and staged, since the sublime is nothing other than a textual performance. What it produces is a reality 'effect', a semblance of the real woven from a tissue of citations. That such a fabrication should compel its readers to embrace a coherent political position, for King, Church and constitution, a position with real effects in the real world, is no doubt astonishing but not all that surprising.

CONCLUSIONS

The Burkean sublime, with its emphasis on the psychological effects of terror, proved decisive in shifting the discourse of the sublime away from the study of natural objects and towards the mind of the spectator. Although Longinus is largely neglected in the *Enquiry*, Burke does show an awareness of the relations between sublimity and language. As Peter de Bolla (1989) argues, whilst Burke makes no overt claims for the discursive origins of the sublime, both the *Enquiry* and the *Reflections* operate beyond the conscious control of their author to suggest this as a possibility. Burke's struggle to maintain the boundaries between words and things is reflected in his treatment of gender and sexuality and, in the field of politics, in his attempts to assert the integrity of a loyalist as opposed to a revolutionary sublime. With Burke we reach the stage where the sureties of the natural sublime can no longer be sustained and where the radical thrust of the Longinian or discursive sublime can no longer be ignored.

4

KANT

THE 'ANALYTIC OF THE SUBLIME'

The 'Analytic of the Sublime', by the German Idealist philosopher Immanuel Kant (1724–1804), is widely held to be the first properly philosophical treatment of the sublime. Published in 1790, the discussion forms the centrepiece of Kant's *Critique of Judgement*, which itself forms the conclusion to a trilogy of works comprising the *Critique of Pure Reason* (1781; revised 1787) and the *Critique of Practical Reason* (1788). In this chapter we will look at how Kant addresses the conceptual problems of eighteenth-century discussions of the sublime. Thereafter, in chapter 5, we will consider the impact of Kant's discussion of the sublime on the development of German Idealist philosophy and British Romantic poetry. Although in recent years it has become unfashionable to link these movements (see Ashfield and de Bolla 1996: 2–3), the parallels between them remain striking and deserving of further commentary. Before embarking on this study, however, we must first establish the basic tenets of Kant's philosophy, paying close attention to its critique of the opposition between empiricism and rationalism. Only then will we be able to appreciate how the 'Analytic of the Sublime' provides a way forward from the conceptual deadlock found in Baillie and Burke.

THE CRITIQUES OF PURE AND PRACTICAL REASON

Kant is a notoriously difficult philosopher to introduce, not least because his complex prose style, even when read in his native German, presents a formidable challenge to conventional notions of ease and understanding. What Kant lacks in fluency, however, is outweighed by his considerable strength as a uniquely subtle, idiosyncratic, and groundbreaking thinker. In this section I will show how Kant builds on the disparate philosophies of the French rationalist René Descartes and the British empiricist David Hume to present what is arguably the first great synthesis of thought in the Western tradition, uniting two opposed schools of enquiry whose origins date back to Plato and Aristotle.

Most accounts of Kant's philosophy note how Kant compares 'his assumption that objects must conform to our cognitions, rather than our cognitions to objects, to the Copernican revolution' (Monk 1960: 4–5). As he writes in the second preface to his *Critique of Pure Reason*, 'the fundamental laws of the motions of the heavenly bodies ... would have remained for ever undiscovered if Copernicus had not dared, in a manner contradictory of the sense, but yet true, to seek the observed movements, not in the heavenly bodies, but in the spectator' (1965: 25). Key to this discovery is Kant's emphasis on the contradiction of the senses and the subsequent shift from the spectacle to the spectator, or from world to mind. Thus, although Kant agrees with Hume 'that all our knowledge begins with experience', he adds that 'it does not follow that it arises out of experience' (1965: 41). Knowledge that does not arise out of experience Kant terms *a priori* (meaning independent or before). The conditions for *a priori* knowledge are necessity and universality. Such knowledge, in other words, must be true at all times and under all conditions, without exception. It is, moreover, not subject to contradiction, in the way that an empirical judgement such as 'the sun will rise tomorrow' (based on previous observation) is. Kant has in mind here the basic truths of mathematics; the proposition '1 + 1 + 1 = 3', for example, is a necessary and universal truth, independent of experience. It cannot be otherwise. In all, Kant identifies twelve such concepts, including time, space, and logic, all of which can be known prior to the experience of nature. But this is not to say that such knowledge is unrelated to experience or, for that matter, that experience can be understood without reference to these concepts. My particular perception, for example, of three trees presupposes the universal, *a priori* concept of number. That is, in order to understand the significance of my raw, unmediated perception (Kant calls this a 'sensible intuition') I must relate it to some pre-existing, i.e. non-empirical, concept, in this case the concept of number. Whilst I am unable to point to or verify the empirical existence of such a category, it must nevertheless be presupposed if my perception is to make sense. As Kant puts it, the 'objective validity of the categories as *a priori* rests, therefore, on the fact that ... through them alone does experience become possible. They relate of necessity and *a priori* to objects of experience, for the reason that only by means of them can any object whatsoever of experience be thought' (1965: 126) or, more simply, 'Thoughts without content are empty; intuitions without concepts are blind' (93).

To establish the underlying *a priori* conditions of knowledge, Kant adopts what he calls a 'transcendental' argument. By transcendental he seeks to convey the sense in which his philosophy aims to uncover the fundamental principles that enable us to make claims about the world. Thinking, in other words, must transcend mere sensible intuitions (the immediate evidence of the senses) so as to establish the existence and nature of the *a priori*. What Kant terms the faculty of understanding is critical to this project. For him the products of sensible intuition, such as feelings of warmth, or hardness, are first of all *synthesized* or represented through the faculty of imagination, then '*thought* through the understanding' (65). The evidence of the senses, in other words, would be meaningless without the harmony of imagination and understanding, which together draw the raw immediacy of nature under the domain of concepts. It is via *a priori* concepts such as time and space that the objectivity of my experience is made possible for me. That such concepts are indeed 'transcendentally ideal' – that is, they have no existence apart from the mind – does not in any way diminish their status as guarantors of empirical existence.

Kant's preoccupation with the interaction of the faculties of sensibility and understanding is supplanted in the second half of the *Critique* by a critical analysis of the faculty of reason. Unlike understanding, pure reason, left to its own, is unable to contribute to the philosophy of knowledge. Where understanding deals with the basic concepts of existence, such as time, space, and number, reason focuses on 'ideas', such as our idea of God, of justice, or of freedom. Unlike the concepts of understanding, such ideas need not be presupposed when attempting to account for experience. The ideas of reason cannot be proved or demonstrated. Yet at the same time they cannot be disproved. In other words 'one cannot have knowledge of the non-existence of such objects' (Burnham 2000: 22). The idea of reason functions negatively therefore in such a way as to expose the limits of understanding. Thus in theoretical physics the notion of unified field theory is posited as the 'Holy Grail' towards which understanding aspires. In this narrow sense, reason allows us to transcend the natural realm and to pursue thought without restriction. The *a priori* principle of the faculty of reason is thus quite simply the *obligation* to think beyond the given. Kantian reason is therefore fundamentally allied with ideas of moral behaviour, with human action that, whilst unrelated to knowledge in the strictest sense, nevertheless contributes to our experience of being in the world.

Kant's ideas about moral actions are developed in the *Critique of Practical Reason*. Like its predecessor the aim of the second *Critique* is to uncover the transcendental conditions for moral or practical behaviour. If, as Kant argues, desire is pure, then it must be founded on an *a priori* principle, which will function independently of any empirical determination. For an action to be moral, that is, it must be guided by a principle that has nothing to do with basic human wants and desires. For Kant, the study of practical reason is thus directed towards the *a priori* that legislates for 'free ethical action: what we ought or ought not to do, but are not compelled to do by any natural condition' (Burnham 2000: 23). Only a moral action that is exempted from natural law, that is free, in other words, with respect to the promptings of desire, can be regarded as truly moral. Here it is important that we grasp the importance that Kant places on this notion of reason. For Kant the purpose of philosophy is not merely to provide a theoretical foundation for knowledge of the world. With respect to reason as a whole, Kant regards epistemology as subordinate to ethics. The aim of a philosophy of knowledge, in other words, is to provide a foundation for a philosophy of the Good. Our freedom, with respect to the contents of our experience, is thus a mere condition for the exercise of moral behaviour.

THE CRITIQUE OF AESTHETIC JUDGEMENT

But if Kant's first *Critique* explores the transcendental conditions of our 'theoretical' understanding of the world, and his second the transcendental conditions underlying our 'practical' or moral activity in this world, the question remains as to how these two approaches to philosophy may be related. The answer to this question is to be found, naturally enough, in the pages of Kant's third *Critique*, the *Critique of Judgement*. But first, what does Kant mean by judgement? As the third faculty, after understanding and reason, the faculty of judgement refers quite simply to our ability to judge things. More specifically, judgement is regarded by Kant as a mediating faculty, one that allows us to link concepts drawn from the other cognitive faculties and to apply them to particular cases. To give an example, a concept such as Pythagoras' theorem, drawn from the faculty of understanding, allows us to legislate on a range of geometrical cases. By applying the general rule to the particular instance, I come to a 'determinate' judgement: the square on the hypotenuse of *this* right-angled triangle is equal to the sum of the squares on the other two sides. By contrast, an 'indeterminate' judgement is one in which the particular case has not been encountered before and for which I am unable to supply a general concept. In all such cases of pure reason, my ability to judge effectively is thus determined by my ability to apply a general concept, which has universal validity and which exists prior to experience. With the appearance of something new in the world, however, be it an unprecedented ethical quandary, the discovery of a new species of plant, or a work of art, we must create a new concept.

Of all so-called 'indeterminate judgements' it is 'aesthetic judgement' that presents the greatest challenge. A judgement of taste such as 'this picture is beautiful' cannot be validated either by reason or by understanding; it is grounded in personal taste and you may well choose to disagree with me. However, Kant argues that despite the fact that such judgements involve personal taste, they nevertheless function *as if* they were statements of fact. In other words, they function *as if* the quality of beauty were a real, objective property of the object judged. Moreover, as Kant argues, due to the fact that the judgement behaves *as if* it were a statement of fact, it demands the agreement of others: 'A judgement of taste requires everyone to assent; and whoever declares something to be beautiful holds that everyone ought to give his approval' (1987: 86)

Still this does not account for disputes about taste. To be sure, my judgement of *Paradise Lost* may demand universal assent, but the fact that people argue about the value of this poem and not about the heat of the sun suggests that it cannot behave in the same way as a simple matter of fact. How, then, are we to account for the universality of aesthetic judgements? Kant's argument at this point is not entirely clear, but in brief it rests on the idea that judgements of taste presuppose a principle of 'common sense' (87). By common sense, Kant does not mean everyday or common knowledge based on experience or pure reason. If I state, for example, that fire is hot, I assume that everyone *will* agree with me. If I state, by contrast, that a poem is beautiful, I state merely that everyone *ought* to agree with me. 'Hence', as Kant argues, 'the common sense, of whose judgement I am at that point offering my judgement of taste as an example ... is a mere ideal standard', not a statement of reason or of fact (89). The *'ought'* in my statement signifies only 'that there is a possibility of reaching such agreement' (90), that there is, in other words, a shared capacity for thinking freely about such matters without reference to determinate concepts or to matters of fact. As Kant summarises: 'for beauty is not a concept of an object, and a judgement of taste is not a cognitive judgement. All it assumes is that we are justified in presupposing universally in all people the same subjective conditions of the power of judgement that we find in ourselves' (156).

THE 'ANALYTIC OF THE SUBLIME'

With the judgement of taste, therefore, the mind is liberated from its dependence on sensuous intuition: an aesthetic judgement is 'pure' precisely because it is not implicated in anything beyond itself. What Kant has to say about the violent or uncontrollable aspects of the sublime appears to contradict this thesis, however. To begin with he notes that the sublime, like the beautiful, does not 'depend upon a sensation' and has an indeterminate relation with concepts. Consequently, as he continues, the delight of the sublime is connected with 'the mere exhibition or power of exhibition, i.e., with the imagination, with the result that we regard this power, when an intuition is given us, as harmonizing with the power of concepts, i.e., the understanding or reason, this harmony furthering [the aims] of these' (1989: 97). In addition, judgements of the sublime and judgements of the beautiful are 'both singular, and both profess to claim universal validity' (Crowther 1989: 79).

Following on from this, however, Kant notes two important differences. In the first case, where the beautiful is concerned with 'the form of an object', with that which is bounded and can thus be distinguished clearly and coherently, the sublime is 'to be found in a formless object ... while yet we add to this *unboundedness* the thought of its totality' (1987: 98). The sublime, in other words, refers to things which appear either formless (a storm at sea; a vast mountain range) or which have form but, for reasons of size, exceed our ability to perceive such form. In either case, the object is considered formless because 'we cannot unify its elements ... in sense intuition' (Crawford 1974: 99). Our ability to discern boundaries or spatial or temporal limitations is brought into question by the sublime. The second, and for Kant most important, distinction is that 'whereas natural beauty' provides judgement with an echo of its own capacity for self-determination, so that nature appears 'preadapted' or 'purposive' to this faculty, the sublime, by contrast, appears to frustrate judgement, to the extent of calling its autonomy into question. The sublime, in short, is presented here as an affront or 'outrage' to our powers of comprehension.

So far, then, what Kant says about the sublime appears to reverse all the claims made in the *Critique* on behalf of the faculty of judgement. In a few moments we will consider how Kant goes on to reassert judgement in the face of this violation. First, however, it is worth attending to his descriptive summary of the feeling of the sublime, which is reminiscent of Burke in its use of physiological and psychological vocabulary:

> The feeling of the sublime is a pleasure that arises only indirectly: it is produced by the feeling of a momentary inhibition of the vital forces followed immediately by an outpouring of them that is all the stronger. Hence it is an emotion, and so it seems to be seriousness, rather than play, in the imagination's activity. Hence, too, this liking is incompatible with charms, and, since the mind is not just attracted by the object but is alternately always repelled as well, the liking for the sublime contains not so much a positive pleasure as rather admiration and respect, and so should be called a negative pleasure.
>
> (98)

Where the beautiful 'carries with it directly a feeling of life's being fur-thered' (98), the sublime, by contrast, involves a suspension of the vital powers; where the apprehension of beauty is straightforwardly appeal-ing, the sublime alternates between attraction and repulsion. Kant, moreover, agrees with Burke in concluding that the sublime is a source of pleasure, albeit of a strictly negative kind. But where Burke links sublime delight with the psychological relief at having survived and managed a life-threatening experience, Kant looks towards more rar-efied horizons. Here again we must keep in mind the rigorously tran-scendental nature of Kant's philosophy: in any philosophical enquiry worth its salt, the point is not to focus on the sensuous or empirical aspects of human existence, for knowledge, in the strict sense, is derived not from the world of experience but rather from the *a priori* conditions of experience. In a judgement of taste, therefore, it is not the object itself that is beautiful but the manner in which the mind apprehends that object, manifesting its accordance with an indeterminate concept of understanding. Like the beautiful, therefore, the sublime is not a prop-erty of nature. Given what has already been said about the sublimity of storms and such like, this might seem nonsensical. But here again we must bear in mind that judgements of taste refer more to subjective conditions of perception than to qualities inherent in the sensuous world.

Still, a distinction must be made between the type of subjectivity involved in the perception of beauty and that which underlies the encounter with the sublime. If the whole point of a judgement of taste is to show how nature and understanding may be brought to a definite end; to show, in other words, how well adapted nature is to the *a priori* condi-tions of subjectivity, then the emphasis Kant places on the ability of the sublime to 'outrage' our powers of perception (more properly identified as the faculty of sensible intuition or imagination) and to 'contravene' judgement seems once again to undermine this point. A hint as to how this problem might be resolved is given in the account of sublime 'delight'. How is it that rational human beings derive pleasure from a painful or life-threatening experience? Whilst psychology, via Burke, goes some way towards answering this question, it is perhaps more inter-esting to observe that in the case of the sublime the feeling of pleasure is unrelated to experience as such. A sublime object may be terrifying, but the fact that I derive pleasure in the contemplation of this object and not pain suggests that my feeling is radically subjective. The object, as it were, no longer has any bearing on my judgement, as it would do in the contemplation of beauty. More so than beauty, the sublime is on the side of mind: 'the sublime, in the proper meaning of the term', writes Kant, 'cannot be contained in any sensible form' (99).

The argument based on the relation of pleasure and pain goes some way towards highlighting the primacy of the mind in its dealings with the sublime. The faculty that provides the *a priori* principle of this delight has not yet been identified, however. We must therefore return to the beginning of the 'Analytic'. Here Kant adds that the effect of *'unboundedness'* in a sublime object is nevertheless accompanied by a 'thought of its totality' (98). In other words, if the initial phase of the sublime 'checks' the ability of the imagination to represent an object and of the understanding to supply a concept, the second phase involves a compensatory movement, one that confirms the mind in its ascendancy over, and autonomy from, nature. Thus, to continue the quotation left suspended at the end of the previous paragraph, 'the sublime cannot be contained in any sensible form' because it 'only concerns ideas of reason, which, though they cannot be exhibited adequately, are aroused and called to mind by this very inadequacy, which can be exhibited in sensibility' (99).

To give an example, in contemplating the stars, the ability of imagination to present an object 'fit' for understanding necessarily fails, yet this does not prevent my sustaining the 'idea' of the universe as infinitely great. The concept of infinity, which belongs properly to reason, is presented negatively by virtue of the inability of imagination to present an object that would be adequate to this concept. The very fact that I can conceive of an infinite universe at the very moment when my imagination fails points to the existence of a faculty completely unrelated to sensuous intuition. This faculty is reason.

We shall return to consider this argument in more detail shortly. First, however, we must attend to an important distinction Kant makes between what he calls the 'mathematical and dynamical sublime'. In the mathematical sublime, the imagination is overwhelmed by spatial or temporal magnitude; the experience is too great for the imagination to 'take it all in' at once (see Burnham 2000: 91). With the dynamical sublime, a sense of overbearing power blocks our will; in the face of this experience the subject is rendered helpless. Of the two types of the sublime it is the mathematical that interests Kant the most. He begins his discussion by offering a broad definition of the sublime: it 'is the name given to ... *what is large* [or great] *beyond all comparison*' (1987: 103). When faced, in other words, with a seemingly endless sequence of sensible intuitions, the imagination is overcome by the impossibility of ever accounting for the sequence in its entirety. If I attempt, for example, to account for the enormity of the Milky Way, I may well begin with a unit of measurement such as the size of my own body and extrapolate from there to gauge the diameter of the earth, the distance from the earth to the sun and the distance from the sun to the nearest star. But whilst it may be possible to calculate the extent of our galaxy using concepts drawn from the faculty of understanding (the category of quantity, for example), my ability to conceive of this measurement in relation to more intimate units of measurement necessarily fails. To go back to the definition given above, the length of my body just does not compare with the enormity of the galaxy. I am simply unable to 'take in' this comparison, just as I am unable to get to grips with the fact that my standard unit of measurement, my body, is made up of millions of cells and countless numbers of atoms. A computer may well present me with a rough estimate of either of these figures, but still, from an aesthetic point of view, I am unable to form a sense of them as real magnitudes (see Crowther 1989: 105–7). 'In each case', as Kant puts it, 'the logical estimation of magnitude progresses without hindrance to infinity' (1987: 111). Infinity, that is, cannot be grasped in sensible intuition, but we can at least think of it as an idea of reason, a point to which we shall return in a moment.

Like the mathematical sublime, the dynamical sublime blocks the ability of the imagination to act in accordance with the understanding. In this case, however, Kant is more obviously concerned with the emotional contours of this experience. Thus he associates the dynamical sublime with fear in the face of the overwhelming forces of nature:

> bold, overhanging and, as it were, threatening rocks, thunderclouds piling up in the sky and moving about accompanied by lightning and thunderclaps, volcanoes with all their destructive power, hurricanes

with all the devastation they leave behind, the boundless ocean heaved up, the high waterfall of a mighty river, and so on. Compared to the might of any of these, our ability to resist becomes a significant trifle.

(120)

Yet here again, the dynamical sublime does not refer strictly to some inherent quality within the object. As Kant continues, 'the sight of [such an object] becomes all the more attractive the more fearful it is, provided we are in a safe place' (120). The dynamical sublime is a source of delight, in other words, because it is contemplated from afar. It is our ability to appreciate our weakness in the face of nature and at the same time to put this weakness into perspective that transfers the attribute of 'mightiness' away from the object and towards something within the mind of the perceiver. Nature thus conceived has 'no dominion over us'. The sight of the 'boundless ocean' may dwarf my imagination, yet my ability to conceive of this deficiency points to the existence of a higher faculty, something greater even than either nature or imagination. As Kant continues:

And we like to call these objects sublime because they raise the soul's fortitude above its usual middle range and allow us to discover in ourselves an ability to resist which is of a quite different kind, and which gives us the courage [to believe] that we could be a match for nature's seeming omnipotence.

(120)

Kant, to reiterate, regards the sublime as an attribute not of nature, but rather of the mind. In the case of the mathematical sublime, it is the ability of the mind to submit formlessness, such as the random, excessive movements of a storm, or the imperceptible contours of a vast cathedral, to the rational idea of *totality*. Through the encounter with the vast in nature the mind discovers within itself a faculty that transcends the realm of sensible intuition. Similarly with the dynamical sublime, in contemplating might from afar, the mind realises the rational idea of *freedom* – from its slavish dependence on nature and the faculty of imagination. In both cases what is uncovered is the rational *a priori* ground of cognition, a pure 'idea' of totality or freedom, which is not subject to the empirical, contingent conditions of nature. Significantly, both realisations arise on the basis of an initial failure in our ability to comprehend. As Kant summarises:

> the feeling of the sublime is a feeling of displeasure that arises from the imagination's inadequacy, in an aesthetic estimation of magnitude, for an estimation by reason, but it is at the same time also a pleasure, aroused by the fact that this very judgement of the inadequacy, namely, that even the greatest power of sensibility is inadequate, is [itself] in harmony with rational ideas, insofar as striving toward them is still a law for us.
>
> (114–15)

The experience of the sublime thus involves a feeling of pain brought about by incapacity of imagination followed 'by a powerful sense of relief (even elation) in so far as the formless phenomenon *can* be grasped as a totality in terms of a rational idea' (Crowther 1989: 81). The failure of 'the greatest faculty of sense' thus serves to 'negatively' exhibit the 'higher' faculty of reason. We get a *feeling*, in other words, for a capacity within our minds that is 'essentially transcendent to (that is, free from) all determinations of nature, inner and outer' (Burnham 2000: 99). The key word here is 'feeling', for were the faculty of reason to be subject to direct empirical presentation it would cease to function as an *a priori* ground for the cognisance of nature in its totality; it would cease, in Kant's words, to be 'pure and independent' (1987: 116). The very fact that we are able to conceive of infinity as a whole, that we are able, in other words, to comprehend ideas which exceed direct empirical presentation, shows that 'we are beings with capacities that transcend the limitations of our finite phenomenal existence' (Crowther 1989: 99–100). Sublimity, therefore, resides in the human capacity to think beyond the bounds of the given.

THE ETHICS OF THE SUBLIME

This brings us to the question of the relation between sublimity and morality. Human beings are liberated from the constraints of nature by their capacity for reason, to think, that is, beyond the limitations afforded by the harmonious interplay of imagination and understanding. With Kant, however, the ability to reason without constraint is not all it appears to be. Reason might be 'free' but this does not mean that we can behave in any way we see fit, in defiance of standard moral laws. Indeed, in the extract quoted above, Kant is at pains to emphasise how reason functions as a 'categorical imperative', a principle that remains true at all times in all circumstances, irrespective of sensible interests (1987: 128). For Kant there is only one categorical imperative and it is this: 'Act only on that maxim through which you can at the same time will that it should become a universal law' (Kant 1972: 84). For example, as a rational being, one cannot *will* that promises are unbinding since, as Kant argues, the universality of the maxim that requires individuals to keep their promises would become impossible (85).

To understand how the concept of the sublime bears on questions of morality we must recall one of the fundamental conditions of the sublime: that it is a quality of mind, not of nature. In other words, in stressing 'freedom' of the will, Kant is not saying 'do as thou wilt', since this implies conformity to natural appetite, but rather 'do as thou should' in accordance with the moral law. The dynamical sublime, in which consciousness realises its independence from nature, thus compels us to sacrifice our pleasures, substituting self-interest for the disinterested love of the good. To give an example, when, in the final scene of the classic film *Casablanca* (1942), Rick (played by Humphrey Bogart) renounces his love for Ilsa (played by Ingrid Bergman) so that she may escape from Nazi-occupied Morocco with her resistance leader husband, he acts against his immediate sensual interests: love, in this case, is supplanted by devotion to a higher Cause. In Kant's terms, Rick's act is sublime because it manifests the ultimate authority and transcendence of the rational over the sensible.

Kant's emphasis on the opposition of reason and self-interest is on a par with what he says elsewhere about the distinction between judgements of the beautiful and judgements of the sublime. In the former, he writes, the mind is 'charmed' by its contemplation of the object; in the latter it is aroused by 'a feeling of respect' (1987: 132), which may even conflict with one's ordinary desires, a classic example of which would be the Christian injunction to abandon even one's family for the sake of truth. Unlike the beautiful, which encourages us to love something apart from self-interest, the sublime encourages us admire something so highly that we would act in defiance of any interest (132). It is beautiful, in other words, to think that we love our children more than we love ourselves; it is sublime to sacrifice one's child for the sake of the truth.

Kant's tenacious insistence on the primacy of truth leads to some disturbing conclusions. Take the injunction against murder. In Toni Morrison's *Beloved* (1987), a novel about the unimaginable traumas of Afro-American history, the central character, Sethe, resorts to desperate measures in order to save her children from slavery: she slits her eldest daughter's throat, attempts to murder her two sons, and threatens to kill her baby. She later states, 'If I hadn't killed her she would have died, and that is something I could not bear to happen to her' (1987: 200). In an interview the author explains that through sacrificing her children, 'Sethe is claiming her role as a parent, claiming the autonomy, the freedom she needs to protect her children and give them some dignity' (1998: 43). The words 'autonomy' and 'freedom' signal that Sethe is attempting through this monstrous act to reclaim a sense of the moral law as that which exists apart from sensible interest. If slavery is understood here as the denial of autonomy, of the right to think for oneself and to assert one's independence from the empirical, then infanticide (literally, the taking away of that which is regarded as the slave master's property) is a means not only of reclaiming identity but also of affirming the transcendental conditions of morality as a law exceeding even one's interests as a parent. In this example the law is affirmed negatively, i.e. by way of the sublime: for Sethe the children of slaves must be killed in order that they might not die.

Kant's interest in the transcendence of desire has clear affinities with the discourse of psychoanalysis. As the literary critic Thomas Weiskel observes, citing Freud, the drama of the sublime is a 'direct inheritance from the Oedipus-complex' (1976: 93–4). Just as, in Burke, the sublime is presented as a struggle between father and son for possession of the mother, so in Kant the conflict between reason and imagination ends with the establishment of a pact: the mind identifies with a higher authority, the faculty of reason, so that it may be delivered from its temptation to fade into sensual or numerical excess. Similarly in Kant's discussion of morality, individual desires must submit to the categorical imperative, even to the point of death, lest ethics be reduced to a matter of taste. As Sethe discovers, the paradox of freedom is dependent on one's willingness to submit to a principle of authority absolutely sundered from the realm of experience. On this basis, a sublime ethics runs the risk of devaluing desire to the point where disinterest shades into cold indifference for the things of this world (see Milbank 2004: 218–20).

THE POLITICS OF THE SUBLIME

The fact that the 'Analytic of the Sublime' was published in the year following the outbreak of the French Revolution may be accidental, but Kant's conclusions do have a bearing on the philosophical significance of this event. To appreciate the political dimensions of the Kantian sublime we must turn to a text dating from 1795, 'An Old Question Raised Again: Is the Human Race Constantly Progressing?' (Part Three of 'The Conflict of the Faculties'). Kant, unlike Burke, writes from a liberal perspective and is thus broadly supportive of the events unfolding in France. He is, however, not so much interested in the politics of the Revolution, as in the feeling it arouses in its spectators:

> The revolution of a gifted people which we have seen unfolding in our day may succeed or miscarry; it may be filled with misery and atrocities to the point that a sensible man, were he boldly to hope to execute it successfully the second time, would never resolve to make the experiment at such cost – this revolution, I say, nonetheless finds in the hearts of all spectators (who are not engaged in the game themselves) a wishful participation that borders closely on enthusiasm, the very expression of which is fraught with danger; this sympathy, therefore, can have no other cause than a moral predisposition in the human race.
>
> (Kant 1963: 144)

For Kant, the Revolution enters the historical arena as a sign of moral progress, irrespective of its practical outcome. What matters here is not the actuality of the Revolution, from the burning of the Bastille, to the execution of the royal family and the descent into terror, but rather its status as an Idea. Let us recall that for Kant, ideas regulate the way we gain knowledge of the world, but cannot themselves be presented. So, for instance, revolution is an idea because 'it cannot be represented as a whole by any object or experience', whereas the fall of the Bastille 'can be identified with a date, a country', and the actions of a group of people. As the critic Simon Malpas explains, such an event 'can be brought under a concept or concepts ... because we have the idea of history to categorise it' (2003: 40). In a further turn, however, the event itself can become a sign for the unpresentable idea of history, in this case the idea of human progress. That the burning of the Bastille and the events that follow should fall short of this idea is to be expected, and this may well be a source of some pain. The enthusiasm generated in the minds of its spectators does, however, testify to the emergence of a secondary feeling of pleasure brought about from the realisation that no phenomenon, no matter how great, can present the Ideas of Reason. The French Revolution is sublime, therefore, because it recalls us to the impossibility of granting sensual form to supersensible ideas.

Ideas of freedom and progress are thus raised above the level of experience. Significantly, however, the feeling for the sublime dimensions of progress is brought about only within the context of an empirical event, i.e. the act of revolution. Just as 'Thoughts without content are empty [and] intuitions without concepts are blind' (Kant 1965: 93), so the transcendental aspect of the political means nothing outside of its concrete realisation. We can conceive of freedom only in the context of history, which amounts to saying that concepts, such as freedom, cannot, in the end, be extracted from real-world experiences.

This points to a significant problem in Kant's reasoning. The sublime belongs to the sphere of reason, yet it is manifested through real-world objects, such as oceans and mountains, and real-world events, such as storms and political revolutions. As the poststructuralist critic Paul de Man argues, Kant is unable to escape the intertwining of the conceptual and the material since the only possible link between these realms is a concept which points to their co-implication. Still more radically, de Man claims that Kant's account of the failure of imagination and the awakening of the mind to the supersensible power of reason is not an 'argument', but a 'story'. As such, 'We are clearly not dealing with mental categories but with tropes and the story Kant tells us is an allegorical fairy tale' (de Man 1990: 104–5). The model that Kant uses to articulate the supersensible is, for de Man, 'no longer properly speaking philosophical, but linguistic. It describes, not a faculty of the mind ... but a potentiality inherent in language' (95). De Man, like de Bolla, refers here to the combinatory power of language, and specifically to the work of metaphor by which one linguistic term is substituted for another. Thus in the case of Kant, imagination is substituted for reason and in such a way as to grant these abstract faculties the power of human agency: the imagination, for example, is said to act in a certain way, as if it possessed free will. The absurdity of this substitution is revealed as soon as it is translated back into the terms of philosophy, at which point 'it loses all inherent coherence' (95). As de Man concludes, the story of reason's triumph over imagination is shown to be dependent on a linguistic structure 'that it not itself accessible to the powers of transcendental philosophy' (95).

To return to Kant's text on the French Revolution, the reason why the spectator's 'wishful participation' should be regarded as a potential 'danger' is that it runs the risk of conflating the empirical and the transcendental. In the shift from sympathy to 'enthusiasm', the difference between subject and object starts to collapse; the act of substitution becomes a material transformation, with the result that the political event is rendered impervious to transcendental critique. Reading via de Man, it is possible to conclude that Kant's text comes perilously close at this point to exposing the linguistic structure on which the drama of substitution depends.

CONCLUSIONS

Unlike its predecessors, the Kantian sublime is presented as neither wholly materialist nor wholly idealist. Rather, it is produced as a structural necessity, a supplement not belonging to the realms of either pure or practical reason, but which yet must be assumed for either to cohere. Sublimity for Kant is the feeling that arises whenever we, as subjects, become aware of the transcendental dimensions of experience. The sublime occurs, that is, whenever ideas exceed the application of a concept; at such moments the mind comes alive to the existence of a faculty of reason transcending the limits of our sensual existence. Contemporary poststructuralist critics such as Paul de Man and Peter de Bolla maintain that the Kantian sublime is nothing more than the effect of the transformational or combinatory power of language. The problem with this approach, however, is that it tends to replicate the very contradictions it sets out to diagnose. As Frances Ferguson argues, 'in making literary or discursive self-reference the central point of the sublime', critics such as de Man and de Bolla assume that 'language is a thing … rather than a medium':

> And the self-reference that language or discourse is able to achieve by virtue of being a thing that is based neither on mind nor on objects ironically recuperates all that was earlier involved in the causal model of relationship between mind and world. Language or discourse is treated as animated matter that produces more of the same by virtue of its inability to coincide with itself (let alone mind and objects), as the spacing within language creates words as separate from one another (and therefore as excess rather than identity) and creates the individual as a subject position, 'an opening within discourse'.
>
> (Ferguson 1992: 19)

Rather ironically, Ferguson concludes, the critique of Kantian idealism, by which the transcendental is reduced to the material, in this case to the materiality of language, ends up repeating the very problem that Kant set out to amend. In chapter 5 we will consider how this problem is taken up in the discourses of German Idealism and British Romanticism.

5

THE ROMANTIC SUBLIME

GERMAN IDEALISM

In the judgement of the sublime, as we have seen, the failure of imagination to fulfil reason's demand arouses in us the feeling, but critically
not the sensual exhibition, of our supersensible 'vocation' (Kant 1987:
114–15). Ideas of reason are represented, therefore, but only negatively: the mind feels but cannot capture its capacity for transcendence. For Kant's followers in the Romantic and Idealist traditions,
this is a particularly troubling conclusion. For what remains, after the
'pleasure' of discovering the non-sensuous, rational foundation of the
mind, is the 'displeasure' of knowing that one can never give sensual
representation to this foundation. Henceforth, in the German Idealist
tradition, the emphasis falls not so much on the triumph of reason as
on the failure of imagination as it strives to realise the ineffable. This
presents a problem for poets and artists striving to defend the primacy
of the imagination. In the case of the poet and philosopher Friedrich
Schiller (1759–1805), for instance, whose short essay 'On The
Sublime' appeared in 1793, the outcome of the sublime is 'a mixed
feeling ... a composition of melancholy ... and of joyousness' (1988:
42). As the literary critic Paul Hamilton comments, 'melancholy
arises from the imagination's loss of its empirical employment'.
Consequently, 'we are no longer at home in the world constituted by
our experience when we are enjoying the feeling of being able to think

beyond it. This joyful feeling of self-aggrandizement defines itself in relation to the unhappy consciousness of no longer belonging to the phenomenal world' (1983: 55).

For poets and thinkers writing in the wake of Kant, then, the sublime induces equal amounts of pleasure and pain: pleasure that the encounter with the sublime should lead to the discovery of a capacity within the self greater than nature; pain at the realisation that such 'power' places us at a remove from nature. Hence the emphasis in German Romantic poetry and art on the desire to overcome the split between the realm of ideas, or noumena, and the realm of nature, or phenomena, from Schiller's *On Naïve and Sentimental Poetry* (1795–6) to F. W. J. von Schelling's *System of Transcendental Idealism* (1800). Schelling (1775–1854) offers a particularly valuable comment on how philosophy might set about healing this division: '[After Kant] nothing remains ... but that [the hidden *a priori* conditions of knowledge] be presented in an immediate intuition; yet this itself seems incomprehensible and ... even self-contradictory' (Simpson 1988: 226). The task, according to Schelling, cannot be accomplished on the basis of philosophy alone. To accomplish the reunion of mind and nature we must draw on the resources made available to us by art: 'For aesthetic intuition is precisely intellectual intuition become objective. The work of art merely reflects to me ... that absolutely identical principle which has already divided itself in the ego' (220). Schelling, in anticipation of Frances Ferguson's critique of de Man and de Bolla, regards the artwork not as a thing but as the medium through which the sensible is reunited with the transcendental. As he continues:

> What we call nature is a poem that lies hidden in a mysterious and marvellous script. Yet if the riddle could reveal itself, we could recognize in it the Odyssey of the spirit which, in a strange delusion, seeking itself, flees itself; for the land of phantasy toward which we aspire gleams through the world of sense only as through a half-transparent mist, only as meaning does through words. When a great painting comes into being it is as though the invisible curtain that separates the real from the ideal world is raised; it is merely the opening through which the characters and places of the world of fantasy, which shimmers only imperfectly through the real world, fully come

upon the stage. Nature [to the artist] ... is merely the imperfect reflection of a world that exists not outside but within him.

(228)

Art, then, has the power to raise 'the whole man ... to a knowledge of
the highest of all' (229). It is art that gives sensuous expression to the
concept of the sublime and which unites the hitherto divided faculties
of reason and imagination.

Schelling's sense of the power of art to manifest the transcendental in
sensuous form is echoed elsewhere in German Romanticism. Thus the
poet and dramatist Johann Wolfgang von Goethe (1749–1832): 'That is
true symbolism, where the more particular represents the more general,
not as a dream or shade, but as a vivid, instantaneous revelation of the
Inscrutable' (Goethe 1893: 102). And now the philosopher, critic, and
writer Friedrich Schlegel (1772–1829):

There is a kind of poetry whose essence lies in the relation between ideal
and real, and which therefore ... should be called transcendental poetry.
It begins in satire in the absolute difference of ideal and real, hovers in
between as elegy, and ends as idyll with the absolute identity of the two.

(Schlegel 1991: 50)

German Romanticism endeavours therefore, in the wake of Kant, to
bridge the gulf between noumena and phenomena, regarding the artistic symbol not merely as analogous to an unknowable idea, of God, for
example, but rather as its 'immediate intuition'. Thus poetry, with its
stress on the synthesizing power of imagination, is given the task of harmonizing the disparate realms of idea and reality, mind and world. In
what amounts to a completion of the Kantian schema, with its emphasis
on the unknowable or hidden grounds of reason, Romantic poetry seeks
to bring the supersensible back into the realm of sensuous representation. Poetry, on this view, will enable us to comprehend the sublime.

COLERIDGE AFTER KANT

The influence of Schelling's revision of Kant was not confined to
Germany. In England, in the aftermath of the French Revolution, writ-

ers such as Samuel Taylor Coleridge, William Wordsworth, William Blake, Percy Bysshe Shelley, John Keats, William Hazlitt, and Thomas De Quincey made similar claims for the primacy of imagination. Like their German counterparts, however, the pioneers of British Romanticism had first to negotiate between the conceptual extremes of empiricism and rationalism.

For one British Romantic writer, the poet, theologian, and philosopher Samuel Taylor Coleridge (1772–1834), the influence of Kant and the German Idealist tradition was to prove decisive. Writing in the *Biographia Literaria* in 1817, Coleridge noted his debt to the 'writings of the illustrious sage of Königsberg', whose works, first encountered in 1799, 'took possession of me as with a giant's hand' (1997a: 89–90). Kant's influence is clearly stated when Coleridge engages with the coruscating logic of Humean scepticism:

> By knowledge *a priori*, we do not mean, that we can know any thing previously to experience, which would be a contradiction in terms; but that having once known it by occasion of experience (i.e. something acting upon us from without) we then know, that it must have pre-existed, or the experience itself would have been impossible. By experience only I know, that I have eyes; but then my reason convinces me, that I must have eyes in order to [have] the experience.
>
> (167)

Here Coleridge avers that the mind is neither reduced to a passing show of sense impressions, as the empiricist Hume had claimed, nor engulfed in an abyss of idealism, as Descartes had implied. For Coleridge as for Kant, mind and world presuppose each other; the one cannot be conceived without the other.

Elsewhere, however, Coleridge seeks to go beyond Kant in his insistence that the unity of mind and world can be intuited as well as conceived. To overcome the residue of dualism in Kant's thought, Coleridge turns, like Schelling, to the primacy of the imagination. His concept of the imagination as 'the living Power and prime Agent of all human perception … a repetition in the finite mind of the eternal act of creation in the infinite I AM' (1997a: 175) is an attempt to yoke the human and the divine, so that higher ideas are not so much represented as repeated in sensuous form. For Coleridge, as for Goethe and Schelling, therefore, 'all our knowledge of God' is not *merely* symbolic but, as it were *vitally* symbolic', so that 'the symbol partakes of the Reality which it renders intelligible; and while it enunciates the whole, abides itself as a living part in that Unity, of which it is the representative' (1972: 30). The word 'symbolic' is used here in a special sense to describe a form of knowledge in which the distinctions between subject and object, self and other, no longer apply. As such the Coleridgean symbol is an attempt to supplant the Kantian privileging of allegory, which, as the historian of ideas Mary Anne Perkins comments, 'merely *points* to a unity of appearance and ideality'. For Coleridge, by contrast, the symbol '*is* an inward unity of the objective reality of the universal idea and the subjective apperception of that reality expressed in particular form' (Perkins 1994: 48–9). His theory of the symbol is an attempt therefore to ally Kantian critical philosophy with the abiding truths of Christianity, so that representation not only mirrors but also participates 'in the nature of the divine Word' (48). Neither thing nor medium, the symbol, like Christ, is a literal embodiment of the word.

In a notebook entry dated April 1805, Coleridge gives practical expression to this idea:

> In looking at the objects of Nature while I am thinking, as at yonder moon dim-glimmering thro' the dewy window-pane, I seem rather to be seeking, as it were *asking*, a symbolical language for something within me that already and forever exists, than observing any new thing. Even when that latter is the case, yet still I have always an obscure feeling as if the new phænomenon were the dim Awakening of a forgotten or hidden Truth of my inner Nature. It is still interesting as a Word, a Symbol!
>
> (1957–90, II: 2546)

The statement exceeds not only Burke, but also Kant, in its insistence on the ability of imagination to regard objects of sense as symbolic of the eternal. Such theory, with its insistence on the creative interplay of experience and ideas, is given practical expression throughout Coleridge's writing, beginning with the religious poetry of the 1790s, "Tis the sublime of man ... to know ourselves / Parts and proportions of one wondrous whole' (from 'Religious Musings', lines 140–3; Coleridge

1997b) and culminating in the philosophical musings of the 1820s: 'Where neither whole nor parts, but unity, as boundless or endless *all-ness* – the Sublime' (quoted in Trott 1998: 85).

Yet as much as Coleridge speaks of a desire 'to destroy the old antithesis of *Words* and *Things* ... elevating, as it were, words into Things, & living Things too' (1956–71, I: 625–6), so that language becomes identical not only with the world of appearances but also with things-in-themselves, elsewhere he maintains fidelity to Kantianism with its emphasis on the strict division between phenomena and noumena. The influence of Kant, as Hamilton argues, is decisive here since it enables Coleridge to develop a theory of poetry in which the poem 'retains its own identity ... distinct from nature, science or anything else' (1983: 62). In simple terms, the wish to extinguish the distinction between poetry and nature, or words and things, is self-defeating since it leads not only to the loss of aesthetic autonomy (the poem as 'self-impassioned') but also to the collapse of the very principle that allows us to apprehend ideas beyond the grasp of understanding. We are no longer able, in other words, to get a sense of concepts 'transgressing the limits of experience'. Sublimity emerges therefore only when noumena are distinguished from phenomena.

The following fragment suggests the extent of Coleridge's affinity with Kant:

I meet, I find the Beautiful – but I give, contribute, or rather attribute the Sublime. No object of Sense is sublime in itself; but only so far as I make it a symbol of some Idea. The circle is a beautiful figure in itself; it becomes sublime, when I contemplate eternity under that figure. The Beautiful is the perfection, the Sublime the suspension, of the comparing Power. Nothing not shapely ... can be called beautiful: nothing that has a shape can be sublime except by metaphor.

(Coleridge 1995: 597)

The first part of the fragment is conventional enough: for Coleridge there can be no 'sense' of the external world 'without the prior participation of the perceiving mind' (de Bolla 1989: 46). Nature, in other words, is re-presented to us as the product of the interaction of mind and object. It is the second part that demands sustained attention. For Coleridge, as for Kant, the sublime is without shape or form; as a thing-in-itself the sublime checks the imagination or 'comparing power', which leads in turn to a suspension of understanding. Yet the sublime may be represented; an object of sense (a mountain, for example) can stand as a metaphor or symbol of the ineffable Idea. The ability of the imagination to inform the sublime, to match a concept with an object, is raised, however, in the full awareness that the object itself is *merely* symbolic. For were the object/image to be regarded, via Schelling, as absolutely identical with the Idea, it would preclude the raising of that minimal distance that allows the mind to become conscious of itself as an entity distinguished from the contents of experience.

The main difference between Kant and Schelling rests on the distinction between knowledge and aesthetics. Where Schelling argues that 'Art', unlike 'Philosophy', 'brings the whole man ... to a knowledge of the highest of all', Kant insists that the sublime cannot become an object of knowledge. Thus whilst it is true to say, with Coleridge, that the poet 'brings the whole soul of man into activity' (1997a: 184), the poet only gives us 'an ideal, imagined sense' of the sublime, 'what Kant describes as an aesthetic idea' (Hamilton 1983: 63). When Coleridge thinks via Kant, therefore, and not via Schelling, he maintains 'that poetry can only *imagine* symbols for such wholeness, and cannot present it to us as part of our knowledge. Poetry gives us an idea which science has not yet realized; but it is an aesthetic idea, "self-impassioned"' (Hamilton 1983: 62; my emphasis). For Kant, the realisation of the distinction between mind and world is something to be not overcome, as it is for Schelling, but rather embraced, for it is only on the basis of this fundamental division that ideas of freedom and autonomy, ideas central to ethical and political life, as well as to poetry, may be asserted.

Coleridge's theory of the sublime is in no way consistent, veering as it does between Kantian, post-Kantian, and British common-sense schools of thought. A poem such as 'The Eolian Harp' (1795; Coleridge 1997b), born out of the Unitarian and pantheistic thinking of the 1790s and subsequently overlaid by the post-Kantian theorising of the *Bibliographia* period, is indicative of this confusion. Yet in many ways it is fruitful to consider the poem as a commentary on Coleridge's endeavour to synthesize a range of competing philosophical attitudes. There is, first of all, the meditation on the harp itself, which, via Kant, becomes a symbol of artistic autonomy, of the work of art distinguished from nature. Still further it lends itself to Schelling's notion of the union of mind and nature, an Idealist thesis ultimately countered by Sara Coleridge's 'look of mild reproof' (line 41). The idea that poetry can ever convey knowledge of the noumenal is exploded in the return to the world of appearance. Ultimately, therefore, the verse returns to the Kantian position that poetry can only ever convey an imagined or ideal sense of the sublime. Thus Coleridge humbles himself before his God, an *a priori* principle, 'INCOMPREHENSIBLE' (line 51) and beyond the reach of concepts of understanding.

Before we go on to consider the development of the sublime in Wordsworth, let us briefly consider a final example from Coleridge's 1818 lecture on 'European Literature':

> But Gothic art is sublime. On entering a cathedral, I am filled with devotion and with awe; I am lost to the actualities that surround me, and my whole being expands into the infinite; earth and air, nature and art, all swell up into eternity, and the only sensible expression left is, 'that I am nothing!'

(Coleridge 2003: 87)

Superficially, this passage resembles Addison with its emphasis on the extinction of the 'I' as it swells and expands into eternity. But where Addison retains a correspondence theory of the relations between objects, ideas, and internal sensations, so that noble buildings, such as temples and cathedrals, 'imprint' the mind 'and fit it to converse with the divinity' (Addison, quoted by de Bolla 1989: 45), with Coleridge there is greater insistence on the sublime as an effect of consciousness. Indeed, as the passage progresses, the concrete reality of the cathedral fades. Notwithstanding the fact that by the end of the second sentence the 'I' is reduced to 'nothing', the overall impression is of a translation of object into subject, of the Gothic church transformed by an operation of mind into a fit emblem of the eternal and thus, by sleight of hand, into a symbol of the unbounded power of imagination.

But how is it that a residue of consciousness survives to proclaim 'I am nothing'? For Peter de Bolla, this remnant of the 'sensible' indicates that the sublime is nothing more than an effect of a metaphoric 'schema' (1989: 47). The fact that the subject who utters this statement is unable to coincide with the subject to whom it applies suggests that the experience of sublime transcendence is purely figurative, a Kantian 'fairy tale' in de Man's sense. Coleridge, however, provides us with an answer to this somewhat despairing conclusion. In a statement on the superiority of poetry to painting, he states that the mind, when

> fixed on one image ... becomes understanding; but while it is unfixed and wavering between them ... [then] it is imagination. The grandest efforts of poetry are where the imagination is called forth, not to produce a distinct form, but a strong working of the mind, still offering what is still repelled, and again creating what is again rejected; the result being what the poet wishes to impress, namely the substitution of a sublime feeling of the unimaginable for a mere image.
>
> (2003: 84)

The inability of language to incarnate meaning in a single image is here celebrated rather than decried. For Coleridge, as for Kant, the 'unimaginable' is that which cannot be submitted to the rule of a concept; it emerges instead as 'a sublime feeling' brought about within the limits of language by the 'working' of a 'strong' mind. There is a sense here, as the philosopher Philippe Lacoue-Labarthe (1989) insists, in which the discourse of the sublime cuts both ways: the interminable 'working' of rejection and creation not only undoes the 'strong' mind, but also gives rise to it, 'since a constitutive openness is precisely what renders it not an object' (Milbank 2004: 212). What prevents the mind, in Coleridge's sense, from collapsing into the materiality of language is precisely the inability of language to coincide with itself. But where Coleridge parts from the poststructuralist thesis is in his conviction that the incompletion of identity is founded, ultimately, on a sense of the divine. For Coleridge, humans are 'spiritual subjects whose Being transcends Space and Time' (Coleridge 2003: 169). The sublime is 'known', therefore, not as an object but rather as a mode of 'elevation', a feeling brought about when the mind encounters the limitations of both 'sense' and 'understanding' (Coleridge 2003: 132; 167).

Let us now see how such feeling emerges in the poetry of Coleridge's friend, William Wordsworth.

WORDSWORTH: STAGING THE SUBLIME

In a passage from his monumental epic of the self, *The Prelude* (1805; Wordsworth 1984), Wordsworth records how, along with his friend Robert Jones, he set out to cross the Simplon Pass between France and Switzerland. Following a break for lunch, the travellers descend to a stream, where the path appears to break off. Unsure of their destination, they proceed upward, but after climbing for some time, beset with 'anxious fears', they begin to realise that they are lost. A chance meeting with a peasant confirms the worst: the travellers have 'crossed the Alps'; attained their goal, in other words, without recognising it as sublime. The 'dull and heavy slackening' which follows this news is 'soon dislodged' (Book 6, lines 549–50), however. For it turns out that the passage is not yet complete; to reach the other side of the Alps the travellers must descend the 'narrow chasm' of the Gondo Gorge. What follows is a marvellous set piece of descriptive sublimity:

> The immeasurable height
> Of woods decaying, never to be decayed,
> The stationary blasts of water-falls,
> And every where along the hollow rent
> Winds thwarting winds, bewildered and forlorn,
> The torrents shooting from the clear blue sky,
> The rocks that muttered close upon our ears,
> Black drizzling crags that spake by the way-side
> As if a voice were in them, the sick sight
> And giddy prospect of the raving stream,
> The unfettered clouds and regions of the heavens,
> Tumult and peace, the darkness and the light
> Were all workings of one mind, the features
> Of the same face, blossoms upon one tree,
> Characters of the great Apocalypse,
> The types and symbols of Eternity,
> Of first and last, and midst, and without end.
>
> (lines 556–72)

As the literary critic Samuel Monk proclaims, the passage 'epitomizes a century of commentary on the religion and poetry in the sublime Alpine landscape' (1960: 227–32). Burnet's distinction between the 'great' and the beautiful, together with his emphasis on the revelatory aspects of mountain prospects, is present here; so too is the 'pleasing terror' of Addison, Dennis, Shaftesbury, Burke, and Thomas Gray (Abrams 1971: 105–7). More profound, however, is the underlying influence of *Paradise Lost* and the Book of Revelation. As the passage concludes, nature is read not only as divine text, but also as a vision of the 'great Apocalypse'. And just as, in the Bible, apocalypse is informed by millennium, so 'Tumult and peace', 'darkness and light', the beautiful and the sublime are regarded as 'workings of one mind, the features / Of the same face, blossoms upon one tree'. The lines end then with an allusion to Adam and Eve's morning song, itself an echo of Revelation, chapter 22 verse 13: 'Him first, him last, him midst, and without end' (Book 5, lines 165; Milton 1980). No other passage in Wordsworth appears so orthodox in its rejection of self-conscious-ness and its embrace of the divine. Just as the processes of nature, the 'decaying' of woods, the 'blasts' of waterfalls, give way to their 'supratemporal' opposites, so the insistent, lyrical 'I', what Keats called Wordsworth's 'egotistical sublime', is displaced by the eternal sights and sounds of God's 'terrible majesty' (see Weiskel 1976: 197–9; *passim*).

And the effect of this vision, as Thomas Weiskel concludes in his landmark study, *The Romantic Sublime* (1976), is not altogether wel-come. Indeed Wordsworth seems unable to integrate his experience with anything that would resemble normal or waking consciousness as, later that night, 'deafened and stunned / By noise of waters' the after-shock of vision makes 'innocent Sleep / Lie melancholy among weary bones' (lines 578–80). As an instance of the 'negative sublime', a sublime exceeding the resources of the self, the passage is without parallel: 'This is simply not the way Wordsworth writes or thinks, not his kind of greatness' (Weiskel 1976: 197). More typical, though no less powerful, is the moving apostrophe to imagination inserted between the prosaic conclusion of line 524 ('we had crossed the Alps') and its resumption at line 549 ('The dull and heavy slackening that ensued'):

Imagination! Lifting up itself
Before the eye and progress of my Song
Like an unfathered vapour; here that Power,
In all the might of its endowments, came
Athwart me; I was lost as in a cloud,
Halted, without a struggle to break through.
And now recovering, to my Soul I say
'I recognise thy glory'. In such strength
Of usurpation, in such visitings
Of awful promise, when the light of sense
Goes out in flashes that have shewn to us
The invisible world, doth Greatness make abode,
There harbours whether we be young or old.
Our destiny, our nature, and our home,
Is with infinitude, and only there;
With hope it is, hope that can never die,
Effort, and expectation, and desire,
And something evermore about to be.

(lines 525–42)

These magnificent lines, perhaps the most closely and appreciatively read in all of Wordsworth's *oeuvre*, provide the poet with abundant recompense for the disappointing encounter with nature. What is sublime, the mature poet realises, is not the grandeur of the Alps, but the 'awful Power' of Imagination. Looking forward to the apocalyptic significance of the Gondo Gorge, the imagination is depicted here as a threatening force, 'an unfathered vapour', strong enough to 'usurp' the 'light of sense'. As such the imagination represents a capacity for excess within the self, a visionary capacity, to be sure, but one that threatens to extinguish not only the evidence of the senses, but also the experience of time and, by extension, the consciousness of self.

As Geoffrey Hartman states, in a reading of this passage from his classic study *Wordsworth's Poetry*, the

original disappointment … suddenly reveals a power – imagination – that could not be satisfied by anything in nature, however sublime. The song's progress comes to a halt because the poet is led beyond

> nature. Unless [the poet] can respect the natural (which includes the temporal) order, his song, at least as narrative, must cease. Here Imagination ... defeats Poetry.
>
> (1971: 46)

To come too close to the sublime is to sacrifice humanity itself. In the lines that follow, Wordsworth initiates recovery by inserting a temporal marker and a locus for his 'unfathered' power: 'And now recovering, to my Soul I say / I recognise thy glory'. The sublime, in other words, is domesticated by means of reflection. Moreover, as the passage proceeds it becomes clear that 'the mind', able to reflect on its capacity for sublimity, is like nature,

> blest in thoughts
> That are their own perfection and reward,
> Strong in itself, and in the access of joy
> Which hides it like the overflowing Nile.
>
> (lines 543–8)

Like Kant's definition of the beautiful, in other words, the Wordsworthian mind is self-contained, serving no other purpose than itself. As Weiskel suggests, the staging of the threat of imagination and its subsequent containment becomes for Wordsworth a means of protecting the self from the perils of the supersensible. For what does the poet encounter in the Gondo Gorge? Could it be that the memory of disappointment is a lure designed to draw attention away from the trauma of having extinguished self-consciousness in the face of infinity? Wordsworth seems driven to exceed 'Nature's littleness', to collapse the self in delirious fusion with Eternity. But he is keen also to restrain this drive; indeed, as we have seen, in the address to Imagination he provides himself and his readers with a key to reconciling what Weiskel calls 'the positive and negative poles of the Romantic sublime' (1976: 204).

The proper movement of the Imagination is therefore 'away from power' and towards a form of 'humanizing' reconciliation. This movement is realised at the end of *The Prelude* following a climactic ascent of Snowdon. Here, Wordsworth presents a vision of the sublime which supports and nurtures the mind, and no longer threatens to annihilate it. It is

> The perfect image of a mighty Mind,
> Of one that feeds upon infinity,
> That is exalted by an under-presence,
> The sense of God, or whatso'er is dim
> Or vast in its own being ...
>
>   (Book 13, lines 69–73)

Such 'Power', Wordsworth concludes, is 'a genuine Counterpart / And Brother of the glorious faculty / Which higher minds bear with them as their own' (lines 88–90). That faculty, called Imagination, is also, in a further, curious echo of Kant, 'but another name ... [for] reason in her most exalted mood' (lines 167–70). Strength therefore resides in our ability to remain at the threshold of the supersensible; to progress beyond this point, to seek to embrace rather than glimpse the promise of 'something evermore about to be' (Book 6, line 542), is to risk descent into the vale of non-sense.

Weiskel's influential reading of the Wordsworthian sublime is avowedly psychoanalytical. Drawing on Freud's claim that 'the categorical imperative in Kant is ... a direct inheritance from the Oedipus-complex', the sublime becomes for Weiskel 'the very moment in which the mind turns within and performs its identification with reason. The sublime recapitulates and thereby re-establishes the oedipus complex' (Weiskel 1976: 93–4). Hence the recurrence within Burke, Kant, and in the work of the major Romantic poets of scenes of conflict, power struggles between warring principles (mind and nature, self and other), which end with the establishment of an Oedipal pact: the mind identifies with a higher authority (reason or God) so that it may be delivered from its temptation to fade into numerical excess (Kant's mathematical sublime), to fall into material chaos (the Gondo Gorge), or to become lost in 'unfathered' Imagination. In each case, 'the moment of blockage', which 'might have been rendered as one of utter self-loss', becomes an opportunity for establishing 'the unitary status of the self' (Hertz 1985: 53). Hence Wordsworth's staging of the encounter with Imagination. Distance from the sublime is attained only at the moment when the poet is able to reflect on this experience, to read this 'Power' as an aspect of the human 'Soul'. The gift of self-consciousness, in other words, is conditional on the acceptance of rational, superegotory controls. There is 'freedom', therefore, but only within limits. With the acceptance of limits comes the claim to fraternity: the mind establishes itself as a 'Brother of the glorious faculty'. It is no longer a rebel son, a rival to paternal power, but a disciplined equal.

As with Coleridge, sublimity on this account is a feeling, distinguished from a concept, which points towards the unimaginable. Wordsworth's claim to 'power' ought not, therefore, as Hertz argues, to be judged solely as a bid for 'the unitary status of the self'. But nor, for that matter, should it be regarded as an attempt to overcome the arbitrary nature of the linguistic sign. Paul de Man, for example, in his readings of *The Prelude* constantly returns to the idea that the poem seeks through metaphors of unity and completion to heal the breach between sign and meaning (see de Man 1983 and 1984). We have seen how, to some extent, this is true of Coleridge. However, we have also noted how Coleridge defines poetry as 'a sublime feeling' for the unimaginable, brought about by the very failure of language to incarnate meaning. The deconstructive reading of the Romantic sublime remains true, therefore, only in so far as language, to adapt Ferguson, is viewed as a thing, rather than as a medium. The Wordsworthian sublime is a case in point. *The Prelude* does not falter before the limits of language; rather it reflects on these limits in order to move beyond them. As these previously quoted lines demonstrate, Wordsworth's sublime consists in the recognition that no single 'image' can incarnate the fullness of being:

> ... workings of one mind, the features
> Of the same face, blossoms upon one tree,
> Characters of the great Apocalypse,
> The types and symbols of Eternity,
> Of first, and last, and midst, and without end.
>   (Book 6, lines 568–72)

As Jon Cook comments, 'each of the phrases in the sequence is both equally apt and equally limited' (1993: 48), and for good reason; for as soon as imagination is identified with language, we are lost without power to break through.

FEMININE DIFFERENCE

The distinction that Burke and Kant established between the bracing austerity of the sublime and the languorous ostentation of the beautiful is recuperated in the writings of male Romanticism. In both cases, the transcendental ego must strive to detach itself from nature, from society, from the emotions, from the body, and above all from the feminine. What Wordsworth, at the close of *The Prelude*, calls 'sovereignty within' (Book 13, line 114) is thus founded on the conversion of sexual difference into spiritual equivalence. If the sublime is to become a 'positive' experience, the mind must successfully discipline not only nature and the Imagination, but also the female other.

Typically, when women are portrayed in male-authored Romantic poems, they are depicted as not only 'mysterious and elusive but inconstant and treacherous – even [their] womb-like dells and havens ultimately lead to death' (Schapiro 1983: 4). One thinks, for example, of Shelley's ambivalent attitude towards the feminine in poems such as 'Alastor' (1816) and 'The Triumph of Life' (1822), Coleridge in 'Christabel' (1798–1801), Keats in 'Lamia' (1820), and Blake in 'The Mental Traveller' (*c.* 1803), all of whom are no less concerned with the threat posed by women to the autonomy and integrity of the masculine ego. Where female attributes are shown in a positive light, they are usually as a projection of male narcissism: the texts of Romanticism are littered with idealised sister lovers. Thus, in 'Tintern Abbey' (1798; Wordsworth 1984) Dorothy functions as a mute guarantor of poetic continuity: 'a mansion for all lovely forms' should the poet's 'genial spirits' fail (lines 114–43, *passim*). Sara Hutchinson in Coleridge's 'Dejection: an Ode' (1802), Emily in Shelley's 'Epipsychidion' (1821), Astarte in Byron's 'Manfred' (1817) perform similar roles. Where women appear in Romantic poetry, therefore, it is either as the discarded material excess of sublime empowerment, a principle of opposition to be resisted, or as the nurturing, beneficent foil to fantasies of narcissistic reintegration.

But what of writing by women? Since Christine Battersby published her incisive study of *Gender and Genius* (1989), readers of Romanticism have become increasingly aware of the institutional contexts within which women's writing is produced and consumed. As Battersby argues, the gendered nature of the sublime and the beautiful effectively debarred women from adopting the sublime as their own. The aesthetic category best suited to the expression of women's experience was, unsurprisingly, the category of the beautiful. With its ideological stress on sociability and the domestic affections, and its stylistic emphasis on the fleeting, the fanciful, and the pathetic, the beautiful was regarded as secondary to the 'manly' vigour and complexity of the sublime. Too sensual to overcome the bonds of nature, too weak to sustain visionary flight, women were seen as unfit subjects for the trials of the sublime. Accordingly, the title of genius, restricted to poets or bards who wrestled with adversity, became an exclusively masculine epithet; a badge of honour doled out only to those fit enough to see through the illusory comforts of nature and the social. In crude terms, the transcendence of the everyday, and the engagement with moral, political, and metaphysical absolutes, was a strictly male affair.

The notion that *all* female writers of the Romantic period acquiesced in the aesthetic qualities ascribed to them by Burke is itself open to the charge of theoretical reduction, however. On the one hand, it assumes that *all* women writers passively accepted their exclusion from the sublime and that they did not engage in visionary trials of their own. On the other, it fails to acknowledge the possibility that women, for reasons of their own, might seek alternatives to the anti-social, violent, and alienating poetics of the masculine sublime. As the feminist critic Anne K. Mellor argues in *Romanticism and Gender*,

> women writers of the Romantic period for the most part foreswore the concern of their male peers with the capacities of the creative imagination, with the limitations of language, with the possibility of transcendence or 'unity of being', with the development of an autonomous self, with political (as opposed to social) revolution, with the role of the creative writer as political leader or religious savior. Instead, women Romantic writers tended to celebrate, not the achievements of the imagination nor the overflow of powerful feelings, but rather the workings of the rational mind, a mind relocated – in a gesture of revolutionary gender implications – in the female as well as the male body.
>
> (1993: 2–3)

We may consider, as example, the novelist, dramatist, poet, and social reformer Hannah More (1745–1833). Writing in 1799, More identifies the sublime with a masculine writing and ideals. In contrast to women's 'intuitive' appreciation of the minute particulars of human nature, men are

> familiarized … with the vast, and the grand, and the interesting: and they think to sanctify these in a way of their own. … These elegant spirits seem to live in a lofty region of their own minds, where they know the multitude cannot soar after them; they derive their grandeur from this elevation, which separates them with the creatures of their imagination, from all ordinary attributes, and all associations of daily occurrence. In this middle region, too high for earth, and too low for heaven; too refined for sense, and too gross for spirit; they keep a magazine of airy speculations, and shining reveries, and puzzling metaphysics; the chief design of which is to drive to a distance, the profane vulgar … .
>
> (quoted in Cole and Swartz 1994: 145)

As Lucinda Cole and Richard G. Swartz observe, in this passage More 'willingly abdicates the sublime to men, but not without challenging the value of both the practice and its practitioners' (145–6). She shows, in other words, how investment in the sublime leads to the neglect of social responsibilities.

In a related manner, the poet Felicia Hemans (1793–1835) portrays the beautiful as deftly subversive of the politics of the sublime. In 'Dartmoor' (1821), for example, she juxtaposes the 'savage grandeur' of war, past and present, with the beauties of nature. Here, as the critic Nanora Sweet suggests, the periodic eruptions of violence, which punctuate history, are displaced through the benign influence of domesticity, which returns like spring to temper winter desolation. Hemans's 'feminine figuration of "Peace" ' is thus used to critique the tendency of tyrants, such as Napoleon, to enact the destructive trails of the sublime in the sphere of actuality (Sweet 1994: 180–1). For Hemans, the privileging of the beautiful is not an escapist fantasy, a distraction from the serious business of politics and history; it is rather a reminder of the politics of the everyday, the condition of 'normal change' which war threatens to disrupt. By drawing attention to the recuperative labours of nature, to 'the wild flowers', which 'in luxuriant beauty' reclaim the monuments of empire, the poet encourages her readers to weigh the contrast between the sublime desolation of war and the beautiful reclamations of peace. Whilst Hemans is by no means a radical poet, she nevertheless gives vent to a specifically feminine concern with the effects of war on the domestic sphere. In doing so she draws attention to the impossibility of separating the discussion of aesthetics from questions of gender and politics.

The resistance to masculine concepts of the sublime which Mellor detects in women's writing of the Romantic period is perhaps most evident in the novel. In the Gothic fictions of Anne Radcliffe (1764–1823), Lady Sydney Morgan (1776–1859) and Susan Ferrier (1782–1854), for example, a connection is made between the sublime and patriarchal tyranny. Set in remote Alpine landscapes or desolate Gothic towers, the plots depict women subjected to and ultimately resisting the exercise of masculine power. More often than not, the villain of these fictions is a male authority figure, a father, priest, or mysterious Count, whose crimes against women may extend to physical violence and even, in the case of the father, to acts of incest. Symbolically, the patriarch signifies the threat of the unbounded masculine ego; the transcendence of natural limits is associated with the violation of ordinary domestic ties and thus with the collapse of society itself. In the novels of Anne Radcliffe, for example, the threat of the masculine sublime is transferred from the rugged Alpine exterior to the confines of the home. As Mellor points out, Radcliffe repeatedly portrays the home as the 'prison' of women, an illusory haven in which wives, mothers, and daughters are routinely subjected to masculine violence (1993: 93). Yet even as Radcliffe critiques the tendency of the sublime to legitimise patriarchal power, she shows too how positive images of the sublime might assist women, enabling them to see in the unbounded majesty of nature a vision of the ideal society: democratic, unrestricted, and above all free from paternal control. Thus in her most popular novel, *The Mysteries of Udolpho* (1794), a vision of the Pyrenees becomes a moment of liberation:

A landscape spread below, whose grandeur awakened all her heart. The consciousness of her prison was lost, while her eyes ranged over the wide and freely-sublime scene without. ... Hither she would

> come, and her soul, refreshed by the views it afforded, would acquire strength to bear her, with equanimity, thro' the persecutions that might await her.
>
> (1980: 90)

With a mind 'thus elevated', the heroine can look upon the 'boasted power of man' with virtuous disdain.

Summarising her argument, Anne Mellor notes how Radcliffe presents an alternative to the 'Oedipal' anxieties of her male Romantic peers. Where the sublime in Burke, Wordsworth, and Coleridge seems to depend on the extinction of feminine difference, for Radcliffe and other female Gothic writers, the contemplation of the sublime leads to an affirmation of the feminine. Rather than battling to the death with a patriarchal rival for possession of the violated mother, the feminine sublime turns on pacific detachment, an awakening to virtue and the ethics of integrity. Thus Mellor:

> ... the [feminine] sublime arouses a sense of personal exaltation, a consciousness of virtue and self-esteem, and hence of tranquillity, a mental freedom from the tyrannies of men and women who are now reduced to impotent insignificance. If the other is beloved, then the experience of the sublime mediates a renewed connection between the lovers grounded in individual integrity, self-esteem, and mutual respect.
>
> (1993: 96)

Here there is no trace of what Weiskel calls the 'negative' sublime, no fear or trembling in the face of mental dissolution; rather, the encounter represents

> an ecstatic experience of co-participation in a nature ... explicitly gender[ed] as female. For [these women writers], this female nature is not an overwhelming power; not even an all-bountiful mother. Instead nature is a female friend, a sister, with whom they share their most intimate experiences and with whom they co-operate in the daily business of life, to the mutual advantage of each.
>
> (97)

Mellor's compelling reading of the female Gothic omits mention of its most ambiguous and, for this reason, most powerful creation. In Mary Shelley's *Frankenstein* (1818), the reader is faced with competing versions of the sublime: on the one hand, Victor Frankenstein seeks, through the creation of a 'perfected' human being, to bypass the limits of our 'faulty' nature (1985: 77). The inference is clear: the 'faulty' is associated with the female reproductive system. That the outcome of this transgression should be a monster is indicative, no doubt, of Shelley's consciousness of the innate error, the hubris, at the core of the masculine sublime. What is clear is that Victor's wish to create a perfect being is prompted by his disdain for society; to the scientist, man is not defined by his social being, but by his capacity for self-determination. To this extent, he echoes the philosophical findings of Kant and his Idealist followers; like them, what Victor craves is a release from nature. The dream of a perfected being is also, then, the dream of a man unfettered by social or biological limits; it is a dream of pure freedom, in the Kantian sense.

When, following the creation of the monster, and his subsequent abandonment, Victor seeks solace in the valley of Chamounix, he is motivated by a desire to 'forget' himself'. For a brief while, the 'sublime and magnificent scenes' of 'maternal Nature ... afforded me the greatest consolation that I was capable of receiving. They elevated me from all littleness of feeling, and although they did not remove my grief, they subdued and tranquillized it' (141–2). Like his male Romantic compatriots, however, Victor is unable to sustain this sense of relief. Nevertheless, over a period of a month he learns to regulate his sense of tranquillity through repeated excursions in the mountains. A topographical rhythm of ascent and descent thus overlays a mental rhythm of 'elevation' and 'dark melancholy', forming a habit with diminishing returns. In the very nadir of despair, Victor attempts an ascent to the summit of Montanvert, recollecting that the sight of 'the tremendous and ever-moving glacier' had once filled him 'with a sublime ecstasy that gave wings to the soul and allowed it to soar from the obscure world to light and joy' (143). Here, once again, though consolation is associated with the influence of a specifically feminised nature, the quest for the sublime must terminate with the transcendence of all such 'natural' obscurity. Above all it must lead away from the realm of the social; as Victor comments, 'the presence of another' at such moments 'would destroy the solitary grandeur of the scene' (143). Fittingly, it is at this precise moment that the hero is confronted with 'the figure of a man' (144), the appearance of whom might be read as the return of the botched social world that philosophical idealism would seek to negate. That the man should turn out to be the monster, one who subsequently complains of his exile from society and of his master's failure to accept responsibility for his creation, is illustrative of the futility and destructiveness of Idealist concepts of freedom (see Ferguson 1992: 106–12). What Shelley shows, through her critique of the masculine sublime, is the difficulty of sustaining a feminist alternative; where Radcliffe envisions release from patriarchal tyranny in the presence of natural grandeur, the landscape of Shelley is marked by 'darkness and distance'; what attracts Victor to this sublime is the way in which it 'continually raises the spectre of the annihilation of the self', while making that annihilation appear more attractive than the loss of freedom encountered by that self on its entry into society.

The notion that female writers of the Romantic period disavowed the darker aspects of the sublime must be qualified, however. In the case of the poet Charlotte Smith (1749–1806), the sublime is frequently evoked as a means of articulating a range of subjective states, which Enlightenment feminists such as Hannah More would deem untenable. Smith's engagement with Goethe's *Sorrows of Young Werther*, a poem linking the quest for freedom and integrity with the rejection of conventional society, allows her to vent a doubly articulated sense of isolation, both as a woman and as a woman poet. Whether the sublime is adopted as a trope of distance and division, linked to a sympathetic portrayal of suicide, as in the sonnets 'Supposed to be Written by Werther' (from *Elegiac Sonnets*, 1786; Wu 1998: 81), or as a bold claim to literary authority, at the opening of her impressive loco-descriptive poem *Beachy Head* (1807; Wu 1998: 110–31), Smith is enabled to explore extreme aspects of the self that the restrictions of Burke and More *et al.* would otherwise deny to her. Through identifying with Werther's negative sublime, his literal desire for self-annihilation, Smith expresses her dissatisfaction with the gentle restrictions of a gendered society. Above all, she shows how the antagonistic, supposedly 'Oedipal' aspects of the sublime may be employed by women to convey dissatisfaction with the given.

As Cole and Swartz (1994) argue, female claims to the sublime must be placed in the context of a wide range of extra-literary factors. In the case of the working-class poet Ann Yearsley (1756–1806), for instance, the sublime is conditioned by a close engagement with the politics of literary culture. Dubbed 'the Bristol milk-woman', following her 'discovery' by Hannah More, Yearsley was marketed to her middle-class audience as a wild, untutored genius, possessed of an innate capacity for poetic feeling. To some extent Yearsley herself colluded in this process. In her poem 'Night. To Stella' (1785), for example, cited by Cole and Swartz (149), she goes to great lengths to apologise to 'Stella' (More) for her 'wilder'd thought, / Uncouth, unciviliz'd and rudely rough' (lines 138–9). By the end of the verse she announces that she has become a convert to More's 'mild rhetoric' and expresses a wish for her patron to 'teach' her 'honest heart to feel more faint, / More moderate' (line 221; lines 213–14). In effect, the poem plays out the patron's desire to transform excess of feeling (the sublime) into gentle sociability (the beautiful). In 'On Mrs. Montagu' (Wu 1998: 154–5), by contrast, Yearsley disclaims against 'arrogant, imperious man', who wrongly assumes that he can 'soar nobler flights, or dare immortal deeds, / Unknown to woman, if she greatly dares / To use the powers assigned her' (lines 5–7). What follows is a carefully wrought passage in which the poet simultaneously asserts and denies her capacity for sublime expression: 'Strong gusts of thought would rise, but rise to die' (line 51). Although Yearsley appears, then, to defer to the respected authority of More and Montagu, arguing that such 'rude ideas' betray the poet's lack of 'liberal converse', she nevertheless lays a claim to an aspect of the sublime that survives the assertion of intellectual deference. For Cole and Swartz, 'the poet's claim to inarticulation – her assertion that "liberal converse" [or instruction] might have preserved her vision from its own demise – is at odds with what her writing actually performs' (1994: 151). When she writes, for example, 'To all the transport the rapt sense can bear; / But all expir'd, for want of powers to speak …' ('On Mrs. Montagu', lines 62–3), Yearsley exhibits a canny sense of the sublime, akin to those moments in Wordsworth when the speaker stakes a claim to the ineffable, despite being unable to put this claim into words. The poem therefore not only speaks of the poet's inability to say what she feels, it also refers

> to a fundamental condition of the transported soul, which cannot help but fail, trapped as it is within the bonds of the material world, but still capable of recognizing that its true home, destiny, and law is the spiritual. Read in this way, Yearsley aggressively assigns herself the ability to recognize the transcendent reality that lies beyond ordinary perception, and therefore beyond the limits of articulation. Her collapse into silence, from this perspective, is a predictable and intrinsic failure of the sublime itself, in which failure, silence, and loss become signs of a higher meaning inaccessible to ordinary minds, and beyond the reach of words.
>
> (Cole and Swartz 1994: 151)

Thus, although Yearsley is often shown distancing herself from the sublime, in accordance with the instructions of More, she nevertheless adopts the underlying structure of the sublime – its stress on baffled aspiration and the recourse to inarticulacy – as a means of converting unlettered weakness into a token of visionary power. It might not be going too far to suggest, in addition to this, that the sublime, with its emphasis on solitude and self-determination, allows Yearsley to distinguish herself from the influence of her learned peers and the identity they have foisted upon her.

CONCLUSIONS

In Romanticism, the discourse of the sublime is developed as a response to the limitations of Burkean empiricism. For Coleridge, writing under the influence of Schelling, sublimity consists in the endeavour to overcome the distinction between words and things. Yet Coleridge also admits that mental freedom is the product of language's inability to coincide with itself. It is at this point that he comes closest to agreeing with Kant. But where Coleridge goes beyond Kant is in his identification of the incompletion of language with the breach between matter and the divine. Elsewhere, in Hartman's reading of Wordsworth, we saw how 'sublime feeling' is generated as a creative response to the dangers of unmediated vision, and how it can be used to answer the 'all or nothing' conclusions of de Manian deconstruction.

Female writing of the Romantic period maintains an ambivalent relation with the concept of the sublime, not least because of its identification with masculine concepts of power and domination. In the examples of Radcliffe, Smith, and Yearsley, however, a feminist appropriation of the sublime leads to the emergence of new modes of transcendence. This suggests that the sublime ought not to be regarded purely as an Oedipal, agonistic, or masculine concept. Nor for that matter should it be solely identified with the desire to manage and maintain a relation with threatening otherness. Charlotte Smith, in particular, seems eager to identify the sublime with the overcoming of restrictions, even to the point of death. The following chapter, on postmodernist responses to the sublime, takes up this theme, and looks at how notions of impossibility and excess are pursued beyond the limits of reason.

6

THE SUBLIME IS NOW
DERRIDA AND LYOTARD

Postmodern culture, which roughly spans the period from the 1940s to the present day (see Connor 1989), takes a lively interest in the sublime. It differs from Romanticism, however, in its sceptical attitude to overarching master concepts, such as nature, reason, or the divine. As the cultural critic Fredric Jameson argues, in his canonical essay 'Postmodernism, or, the Cultural Logic of Late Capitalism' (1984), postmodernism is characterised by its rejection of systematic philosophies, by its abandonment of authenticity and expressionism, and by its subsequent investment in arbitrariness, artificiality, and 'the waning of affect' (1991: 16). As far as sublimity is concerned, whilst postmodernism retains the Romantic feeling for the vast and the unlimited, it no longer seeks to temper this feeling through reference to a higher faculty. The postmodern condition therefore lays stress on the inability of art or reason to bring the vast and the unlimited to account. In what amounts to a retreat from the promise of enlightenment, its dream of freedom and transcendence, the postmodern affirms nothing beyond its own failure, and it does so without regret and without longing. Postmodernism therefore avoids not only the Romantic belief in the ability of art to synthesise noumena and phenomena, but also the modernist attitude of mourning for the loss of this belief.

The difference between Romanticism, modernism, and postmodernism can therefore be measured in their contrasting attitudes to the unpresentable. Where Romantic art tends, on the whole, to link the unpresentable with ideas of the divine or, in its humanist manifestation, with the concept of mind, postmodern culture endeavours to retain a sense of the unpresentable as absolutely other. It seeks, as the French theorist Jean-François Lyotard argues, to sustain 'the incommensurability of reality to concept which is implied in the Kantian philosophy of the mind' (1984: 79). Postmodernism, as Lyotard sees it, is not a deviation from but rather a radicalisation of Kant's original 'Analytic'; it aims to maintain the shock of the sublime so as to prevent the ascendancy of the rational over the real (see Hamilton 1999: 17). Unlike modernism, therefore, which 'allows the unpresentable to be put forward only as the missing contents', Lyotard claims that the postmodern 'puts forward the unpresentable in presentation itself' (1984: 81). To this end, the art of the postmodern 'denies itself the solace of good forms, the consensus of taste which would make it possible to share collectively the nostalgia for the unattainable ... [it] searches for new presentations, not in order to enjoy them but in order to impart a stronger sense of the unpresentable' (81). In painting, for example, the ultimate mode of expression will be pure abstraction: 'it will be "white"', Lyotard states, 'like one of Malevitch's squares; it will enable us to see only by making it impossible to see; it will please only by causing pain' (78).

Jacques Derrida's work on the concept of the sublime is similarly indebted to Kant. Like Lyotard, Derrida in *The Truth in Painting* (1978; 1987) encourages us to re-read Kant, not as a proto-Romantic thinker but rather as our contemporary, as a post-Romantic theorist for whom the drive towards transcendence is conditioned and facilitated by the limits of the conceptual 'system' in which it is expressed. There is no sublime, in other words, that does not confirm the necessity of conceptual boundaries, no impulse towards the ineffable that does not bear the imprint of contrivance. Here we see, in a nutshell, Derrida's deconstructive methodology by which the truth claims of texts are traced back to a point of fundamental contradiction or paradox. In his reading of Kant, for example, Derrida demonstrates 'the necessary co-implication of the empirical and the transcendental: the transcendental, for instance, never quite managing to pull itself clear of the empirical, and the empirical never quite free of traces of the transcendental' (Maclachlan 2004: 1–2). Lyotard's approach to the postmodern sublime owes much to this deconstructive approach; let us begin therefore by looking more closely at how Derrida pursues Kant in *The Truth in Painting*.

DERRIDA: *THE TRUTH IN PAINTING*

Derrida's analysis of the Kantian sublime hinges on a fleeting reference in the third *Critique* to the concept of the *parergon*. *Parergon* has several meanings, including 'frame', 'addition', and 'remainder'. Derrida begins by citing some of Kant's own examples, such as 'picture frames, or drapery on statues, or colonnades around magnificent buildings' (Kant 1987: 72). In each case, the *parergon* appears to fulfil no intrinsic function; its status is merely decorative. Derrida, nevertheless, goes on to conclude something far more radical than this, arguing that

> what constitutes them as *parerga* is not simply their exteriority as surplus, it is the internal structural link which rivets them to the lack in the interior of the *ergon* [or work]. ... Without this lack, the ergon would have no need of a *parergon*. [But] the *ergon*'s lack is the lack of a *parergon*.
>
> (1987: 59–60)

Why do art works require frames? It is impossible to imagine a painting, for example, without one; even the edge of the canvas marks a limit. And the frame does not have to be physical. Art is defined by its institutional context: a bottle rack, for instance, is just a bottle rack when it is located in a bar. If the bottle rack is removed by an artist such as Marcel Duchamp (1887–1968) and transferred to the setting of a gallery and then given a title, it is regarded as a work of art. The *parergon*, as frame, drapery, column, title, or institution, is not therefore simply peripheral; rather it is directly related to the lack in the interior of the *ergon*.

In the 'Analytic of the Sublime', Kant links the beautiful with the bounded. A beautiful object has clear outlines and distinct form, whereas the sublime is found in formlessness. Derrida concludes, on the basis of this, that 'there cannot, it seems, be a *parergon* for the sublime' (1987: 127). But as the critic Mark Cheetham notes, Derrida's 'seems' offers the possibility that the sublime is bounded, and in ways that fundamentally unsettle Romantic notions of the sublime as wholly other or beyond (2001: 97). To understand this idea it is helpful to recall Kant's arguments for the priority of reason over imagination. In the case of the pyramids, Kant suggests that the sublime emerges only when viewed from a certain point: if too far away, 'then the apprehended parts ... are presented only obscurely ... and if one gets too close, then the eye needs some time to complete the apprehension from the base to the peak' (1987: 108). The sublime, therefore, is an effect of a precise form of alignment; for the mathematically sublime to be produced in us we must first establish a conceptual frame or *parergon*. Reason must step in, in other words, to control the excesses of 'raw nature'. The claim extends to the realm of ideas. Imagination, on its own, is unable to comprehend the concept of infinity. Yet this very failure to present the infinite is nevertheless presented. The question is how? The answer, as Derrida summarises, is that since the sublime 'is not contained in a finite natural or artificial object', it must be sought, rather, in that which has no boundary. The failure of the imagination to present a case for the concept of infinity is thus presented or 'bounded' by the 'unbounded' power of reason (Derrida 1987: 131). It is 'the ability thus to present our very inability to comprehend' that constitutes the true sublime (Cheetham 2001: 106). As Cheetham concludes: 'What would seem to be the limitless power of the imagination and the confined exercise of reason reverse their roles and relative strengths; *ergon* can become *parergon* and vice versa' (106). The pleasure that arises from the sublime consists, therefore, precisely in the setting of, rather than the overcoming of, limits, for reason, unlike imagination,

> can put such a border in place and take emotional pleasure from this accomplishment. That pleasure – not the glimmering awareness of something incommensurably 'other' – is the sublime for both Kant and Derrida. The experience and pleasure of the sublime do not stem from the promise of something noumenal, outside a given frame, but rather from the perpetual, yet always provisional, activity of framing itself, from the *parergon*.
>
> (107)

Consider again the Latin roots of the sublime: *sub* (up to) and *limen* (lintel, literally the top piece of a door). Etymology itself suggests that there is no sense of the unbounded that does not make reference to the placing of a limit or threshold. Yet, by the same token, there is no limit which does not assume the existence of the unlimited. As Kant argues throughout his philosophy, the field of practical reason, which consists in our ability to think and act freely, cannot function unless we presuppose the existence of pure or theoretical reason, a sphere of knowledge that is *a priori* or supersensible.

Our feeling of the sublime, therefore, cuts both ways. On the one hand, it sets a limit through its presentation of the failure of imagination; on the other, it shows how this limit is, in turn, framed or bounded by the unlimited power of reason. In Kantian terms, it might be helpful to conceive of the sublime as a doorway linking the disparate yet interconnected realms of pure and practical reason. Seen from either side, the beyond of reason is thus necessarily 'framed'. It would be impossible to conceive of the unlimited without the limited, and vice versa. For the philosopher Rudolphe Gasché, the sublime is thus 'to be understood as the minimal synthesis in order for there to be a mediation between concepts of nature and concepts of freedom' (1990: 112–13).

This emphasis on the use of the sublime within theoretical discourse marks a turn away from the Romantic emphasis on sublimity as the religious or noumenal 'other' of human conception. For Derrida, as for Kant, the pleasure of the sublime does not consist in the revelation to consciousness of some absolute beyond, but in the recognition that the sensation of the beyond is ultimately an effect of consciousness itself. Where Derrida goes further than Kant, however, is in suggesting that consciousness in turn may be nothing more than an effect of sublime discourse. By reading Kant in a certain way, Derrida, in advance of de Man and de Bolla, insists that reason's rise to supremacy, and the subsequent deification of mind, consciousness, or subjectivity in his thought, is a form of structural blip, a happy accident brought about through the mere workings of a philosophical 'system'. Thus Derrida concludes that the sublime is a double operation, 'both limited since what is presented remains too large ... and unlimited by the very thing it presents or which presents *itself* in it'. Since this double operation 'is compared only with itself', i.e. it has no supersensible or extra-discursive origin, the limit as such 'does not exist' (1987: 144–5).

As I noted at the conclusion of chapter 4, Frances Ferguson, in *Solitude and the Sublime* (1992), takes Derrida and de Bolla to task for regarding language as a thing rather than as a medium. In her view, poststructuralism thus repeats the errors of empiricism in so far as it denies the theoretical necessity of the noumena. Yet while Ferguson's desire to retain the Idealist edge of Kant's work seems, to my mind, to be correct, she perhaps goes too far in her claims against Derrida, for Derrida, no less than Ferguson, is in tune with Kant's own insistence on the sublime as neither wholly materialist nor wholly Idealist in orientation (see Bernstein 1992: 171). Rather, the sublime is produced within the Kantian text as a structural necessity, a supplement belonging to the realms of neither pure nor practical reason, which yet must be assumed for either to cohere. That the sublime should not be pure or practical, formal or material, outside or inside, suggests again that it is a framing effect, itself a *parergon* arising from and intimately linked with the lack that is at the heart of the Kantian project.

To summarise, Kant's brief discourse on the *parergon*, which itself functions as a *parergon* or supplement to the core of his argument, is shown by Derrida to be central to both the formation and the *de*formation of the sublime. The *parergon*, in other words, is that which cannot be thought within the terms of the system since it discloses the fundamental point of contradiction on which the system is founded; it renders the sublime both possible and impossible. It follows that the transcendental dimensions of the sublime, its manifestation of the supersensible, for instance, are never more than '*quasi*-transcendental' (see Bennington and Derrida 1993: 267–84). For Derrida, the Kantian sense of the beyond is therefore an illusion, the by-product of a philosophical system.

LYOTARD

NEWMAN AND LYOTARD: THE POSTMODERN SUBLIME

Let us begin this section on Lyotard by looking, first of all, at the influential work of the American abstract painter and art theorist Barnett Baruch Newman (1905–70). Newman is well known as a

painter and theorist of the sublime. At first glance his work is decep-
tively simple: large, asymmetrical blocks of colour divided by thin
rectilinear lines, which the artist later referred to as 'zips'. The scale of
the canvas, as one might expect, is vast. *Vir Heroicus Sublimis*, completed in 1950–1, measures 2.42 m by 5.42 m. Unlike the virulent,
expressive style of the similarly expansive Pollock, however,
Newman's work is notable for its minimalist restraint. Colour is
applied smoothly and evenly to the canvas, with subtle variations in
tone and intensity. Unlike a realist painting there is, as Lyotard points
out in his essay 'Newman: The Instant' (1984), 'almost nothing to
"consume"' (1989: 241–2). Yet despite the coolness of the artist's
approach, the impact on the viewer is mesmerising. The large blocks
of colour, divided by the contrasting vertical zips, draw the eye into
the canvas, to the point where it becomes impossible to distinguish
between object and subject: the inside of the painting, the *ergon*, and
the outside, or *parergon*, in which it occurs. For Newman, the effect of
this warping of time and space is profoundly spiritual. As he writes in
his influential essay 'The Sublime is Now' (1948), the intention is to
'reassert ... man's natural desire for the exalted, for a concern with our
relationship to the absolute emotions' (1990: 170–3).

Newman's concern with the 'now' is signalled by the titles of his
works, all dating from the early 1960s: his first three sculptures, *Here I,
Here II, Here III*, a painting entitled *Not Over There, Here*, two paintings
called *Now*, and two others entitled *Be*. Such concern with the here and
now appears, at first, to run counter to the spirit of the sublime. As
Lyotard observes in his essay 'The Sublime and the Avant-Garde'
(1984), 'isn't it essential to [the feeling of the sublime] that it alludes to
something which can't be shown, or presented?' (1989: 196). Newman,
unlike Turner, for example, does not gesture towards anything beyond
the work; there is no hidden depth, and no complex meaning to be deci-
phered; its subject matter is itself. In what sense, therefore, can it be
described as sublime?

To answer this question, we should try to imagine a painting such as
Adam (1951–2) devoid of its zips. In the absence of any form of distinction, the experience of a pure colour field overwhelms the viewer to the
point of paralysis. In Burke's sense, the experience is 'terrible' in that it
announces that language, otherness, or life itself will soon be over. 'One

feels', as Lyotard puts it in 'Newman: The Instant', 'that it is possible that soon nothing more will take place' (1989: 245). The painting ushers in a universe of death with no promise of restitution, and, moreover there is no pleasure to this experience. For pleasure to be produced something must be held back; the threat of annihilation must be suspended. Burke, we should recall, uses the word 'delight' to describe the feeling of relief that arises when we become aware of our preservation from extinction. With Newman this delight is twofold. In one sense, the zip functions as a Derridean frame or borderline, dividing order from chaos, enabling us to take a measure of the sublime. In connection with this idea it is helpful to consider that Newman created his lines by applying tape to the ground of his painting, which he then overpainted, removing the tape only when the work was complete. The distinction between the large colour blocks takes place in a dramatic burst of energy, which Lyotard terms the act or event. Just as the finger of God energizes Adam on the ceiling of the Sistine Chapel, so the zip 'descends like a thunderbolt. ... The work rises up ... in an instant, but the flash of the instant strikes it like a minimal command: Be' (Lyotard 1989: 249). Whilst the Derridean frame points merely to the formal nature of the distinction between the sensible and the supersensible, Newman's lightning flash leaves us with a profound sense of its fragility, of a sense of being teetering on the edge of nothingness. The boundary separating something from nothing, the pleasure of creation from the terror of privation, is slight, but it is enough, according to Lyotard, to make us feel the sublime (1989: 204–5).

The stress on the event is important here, since Newman's art exists, according to Lyotard, to prevent the sublime succumbing to the domesticating effects of time and sensibility. As Simon Malpas explains, with Newman the viewer is confronted with an event that resists the imposition of rules and categories. All we know is that 'something happens', but we are unable to decide 'what happens'. For Lyotard, the difference between 'something happens' and 'what happens' is crucial. On the one hand, when we declare 'what happens', we supply the sublime event or object with a concept and thereby shut down its capacity for transformation. On the other hand, if we remain open to the 'something happens', then we maintain the specificity of the event and respond with openness to the challenge of its radical indeterminacy. The sublimity of

Newman's painting consists, therefore, 'in the perception of an instant in which something happens to which we are called to respond without knowing in advance ... [how] to respond' (see Malpas 2003: 101).

The larger implications of Lyotard's theorising on the sublime are explored in 'Answering the Question: What is Postmodernism?' (1984). In this classic essay, Lyotard defines postmodernism as an event rather than as a movement or a passage of time. Like Newman's painting, in other words, postmodernity does not work to confirm the familiar or to reveal the transcendental but rather to precipitate the emergence of the 'now'. Whenever, that is, modernity stalls in nostalgic reverie for the lost contents of the sublime, offering to the reader or viewer the promise of some ultimate 'reconciliation of the concept and the sensible' (81–2), it is then that the postmodern arises to impart a stronger sense of the impossibility of this task.

As illustration of his argument, Lyotard highlights a number of contrasts in the evolution of modernity: between the melancholia of the German Expressionists, on the one hand, and the quixotic inventiveness of Braque and Picasso, on the other; between the reconciliatory aesthetics of Marcel Proust's *A la recherche du temps perdu* (1913–27) and the disruptive *novatio* of James Joyce's *Ulysses* (1922). Where the former 'allows the unpresentable to be put forward only as the missing contents', while its form 'continues to offer the reader or viewer matter for solace or pleasure', the latter 'puts forward the unpresentable in presentation itself'. With its stress on the disunity of form and content, on the arbitrariness of signifier and signified, and on the excessive nature of the Idea in relation to its sensible configuration, the postmodern work effectively destroys 'the consensus of taste which would make it possible to share collectively the nostalgia for the unattainable' (81). The sublime, in a later articulation, is thus 'like lightning' in so far as it 'short-circuits thinking with itself' (1994: 54), exposing 'a basic incommensurability within our experience that neither reason nor understanding is capable of resolving' (Sim 1996: 101–2).

In contrast to the aesthetics of the beautiful, with its stress on the 'unity of experience' (Lyotard 1984: 72), the sublime demands that we acknowledge the absurdity of spanning the gulf between the theoretical and the practical. It does so, Lyotard argues, by retaining the idea of the sublime as an indeterminate 'event'. In terms of what Paul Hamilton calls 'the tense logics of the sublime', our judgement of this event 'is always one of what "will have been", future-perfect, never one which provides a rule for the present' (1999: 17; Lyotard 1984: 81). This is where Lyotard departs from Kant, for it is the purpose of the 'Analytic' to submit the sublime to the discipline of reason, which always arrives, belatedly as it were, to pronounce its judgement. But with the postmodern sublime, judgement is kept open and the specificity of the event is sustained.

In 'After the Sublime: The State of Aesthetics', a paper delivered towards the end of his career, Lyotard approaches the 'something happens' in terms of the relation between form and matter. Arguing once again by way of Kant, he observes that the art of the beautiful is concerned with producing 'data that can be grasped by sensibility and that are intelligible to understanding'. To fulfil this requirement a painting, for example, will endeavour to supply chaotic 'matter' with the harmony of 'form'. By contrast, in the experience of the sublime, matter is invoked in a way 'that is not finalized, not destined'. Sublime matter is that which resists the imposition of forms and concepts. As Lyotard goes on to explain, 'The paradox of art "after the sublime" is that it turns towards a thing which does not turn itself towards the mind' (1991: 141–2). Paradoxically, sublime matter is therefore "immaterial" in so far as an object or thing becomes material only when subjected to the operation of the mind: 'For forms and concepts are constitutive of objects, they pro-duce data that can be grasped by sensibility and that are intelligible to the understanding. ... The matter I'm talking about is "immaterial", an-objectable, because it can only "take place" or find its occasion at the price of suspending these active powers of the mind' (140).

'THE SIGN OF HISTORY'

'Answering the Question: What is Postmodernism?' concludes with the following proclamation:

> The nineteenth and twentieth centuries have given us as much terror as we can take. We have paid a high enough price for the nostalgia of the whole and the one, for the reconciliation of the concept and the

sensible, of the transparent and the communicable experience. Under the general demand for slackening and for appeasement, we can hear the mutterings of the desire for a return to terror, for the realization of the fantasy to seize reality. The answer is: Let us wage a war on totality; let us be witnesses to the unpresentable; let us activate the differences in order to save the honour of the name.

(1984: 81–2)

It may seem strange that a treatise on aesthetics should conclude with what appears to be a clarion call for violent revolution. But as we have seen throughout this book, the discourse of the sublime tends to spill over into other areas of thought. Lyotard, for example, regards the artistic avant-garde as a vital tool in exposing the logic of late capitalism, arguing that the resistance of 'difficult' forms of art to public consensus marks the limits of a consumer-based society. The call to 'wage war on totality' is thus driven by a desire to disrupt the means by which capitalist economies determine reality. The artistic category that Lyotard assigns to the business of forging consensus is the beautiful. With its fostering of unity, harmony, and communicability, the beautiful becomes the perfect form for consolidating the version of reality that best suits the needs of a capitalist regime.

The aesthetic is political, therefore. But how, precisely, does the aesthetic become political, and what bearing does this have on our understanding of the sublime? The answer to both questions turns on our response to a third: how does politics make use of aesthetics? Let us approach this question by way of Kant. In the third *Critique*, Kant distinguishes reflective judgements from empirical judgements on the grounds that the former are indeterminate: that is, reflective judgements, such as judgements of taste, 'have no determinate concept available to them, no universal rule under which to subsume the particular that is given to us in intuition; rather, they try to *find* such a universal' (Kant 1987: lvi). A society endeavouring to present itself as just or good must therefore acknowledge that its relation with these concepts is reflective and indeterminate.

It is when indeterminate judgements are applied to the political, and treated as if they were determinate, that disaster occurs. In *Just Gaming* (1985), for example, Lyotard argues that the injustice and terror of totalitarianism proceeds directly from the assumption that the true, which refers to a determinate object of cognition, and the just, which refers to an indeterminate idea, may be united (see Readings 1991: 108). The 'nostalgia for the whole and the one' leads ultimately to a political desire for the unity of the object and the idea, a desire which, as we have seen, runs counter to the spirit of the sublime (see Lyotard 1985: 22–3). Any society claiming to embody the idea of the just is immediately unjust, for it precludes the possibility of dissent. For politics to be just, therefore, it must strive to affirm the idea of the just as 'unpresentable'. With reference to the 'tense logic' of the sublime, this would involve a commitment to justice as that which remains always to be determined. Like the judgement of taste, political judgement, in this ideal sense, proceeds without reference to concepts; it operates, like the artistic avant-garde, 'as the site of invention, where desire works free of the rule of truth' (see Readings 1991: 72). Here, Lyotard once again goes beyond Kant in seeking to maintain an attitude of suspicion towards all universals, all rules that would legitimize a right to speak in the name of the rational and the real.

Lyotard claims elsewhere that there is no such thing as a politics of the sublime: 'As for a politics of the sublime. ... It could only be Terror.' Terror, let us recall, is linked with privation: 'privation of light, terror of darkness; privation of others, terror of solitude; privation of language; terror of silence; privation of objects, terror of emptiness; privation of life, terror of death. What is terrifying is that the *It happens that* does not happen, that is stops happening' (1989: 204). In the terror of Nazism, for example, the spectator is struck with astonishment, is rendered 'dumb, immobilized, [and] as good as dead' (204). A politics of the sublime, such as Nazism, may be countered, however, by what Lyotard calls 'an aesthetic of the sublime in politics' (1992: 85). Such an aesthetic would operate on the understanding that for 'Ideas, there are no presentable objects – there are only *analoga*, signs, hypotyposes' (84).

Lyotard explains the distinction between judgements by objects and judgement by analogy (*analoga*), in 'The Sign of History', a paper dating from 1982 (see Lyotard 1987) and reprinted in revised form in *The Differend* (1983; 1988): 'When we are dealing with Ideas ... in which intuition cannot, by definition, present anything as an object, presentation takes place indirectly by analogy.' The idea is judged, in other words, 'as if' it were a concept of understanding (1987: 165). Thus the idea of God is explained by reference to the concept of the Father, and the idea of transcendental freedom by reference to the struggle for political liberty. In this way the critical philosopher can continue to make judgements, 'even when there is no empirical case directly presentable for its validation' (165).

How, then, should we set about judging a political event such as the French Revolution? In chapter 4 we saw how Kant addresses this issue, arguing that the Revolution 'arouses in the heart of all spectators (who are not themselves caught up in it) a taking of sides according to desires which border on enthusiasm' (Lyotard 1987: 170). What the spectators see in the revolutionary event is a manifestation of the transcendental idea of human progress. The enthusiasm they feel 'is a modality of the sublime feeling' by which, in Lyotard's terms, we are called to supply 'a presentation for the unpresentable and thus, in terms of Ideas, to go beyond anything that can be presented' (172). The formlessness of the Revolution renders the event resistant to all forms of presentation, 'even', Lyotard adds, 'by *analoga*' (174). All that we have to indicate the idea of human progress is the enthusiasm of the Revolution's spectators, their feeling functions as an 'as if' presentation 'where however there can be no such presentation in experience. This', Lyotard adds, 'is how the sublime feeling is a sign. The sign does no more than indicate a free causality', the ability of a people to think without reference to determinate concepts, 'but it nevertheless counts as proof for the phrase affirming progress: since spectating mankind must already have made progress in culture to be able to feel this feeling, or in other words to make this sign, by "its way of thinking" the Revolution' (176–7).

What would be a sign for our times? Towards the end of 'The Sign of History', Lyotard points to 'a new type of sublime, more paradoxical still than that of enthusiasm, a sublime in which we would feel not only the irremediable gap between an Idea and what presents itself to "realise" that Idea, but also the gap between the various families of phrases and their respective legitimate presentations' (1987: 178). In this new formulation, Lyotard depicts the sublime as an event enmeshed in language. How, for example, should we speak of the terrors of recent history, of Auschwitz, Hiroshima, Cambodia, Rwanda, and 9/11? How could these events be described as evidence of human progress, still less as objects of sublime delight?

Lyotard addresses these questions in his most complex and philosophically sustained work, *The Differend*. He opens this book with a definition: 'In the differend', Lyotard explains, 'something "asks" to be put into phrases and suffers from the wrong of not being able to be put into phrases right away' (1988: 13). An event such as the Holocaust is a case in point. All attempts to give voice to this event necessarily fail since, at present, no idiom exists by which to do it justice. In terms of the sublime, the pain of the Holocaust is such that it exceeds our ability to supply a concept (88). Yet, Lyotard argues, the surrounding silence functions as a sign that 'something remains to be phrased ... which is not determined' (57). Just as, in the feeling of the sublime, the supersensible is capable only of negative representation, so the Holocaust is known only by what it leaves in abeyance. To do justice to the Holocaust, therefore, one must phrase the event in such a way that it remains open to future determination since to do otherwise would be to assume that one has already understood the event and thus consumed it as an object of knowledge. Paradoxically, the Holocaust is 'known' only by refusing to phrase it in terms of a judgement of understanding; for what the Holocaust signifies is nothing less than the impossibility of such knowledge.

THE RETURN OF TERROR

In light of *The Differend* how should we approach the terrorist attack on the Twin Towers? The question is not as simple as it appears. For one thing it presupposes the existence of a worldwide community, a *sensus communis*, to whom such an event could appear as an object of cognition. If there is a politics of the sublime surrounding 9/11 it resides precisely in the feeling that 'we' can no longer speak for the rest of the world. What we can speak of, however, is the feeling that surrounds this event. As Margaret Weigel explains in her article 'Terrorism and the Sublime, Or Why We Keep Watching' (2001), the reason why spectators around the world compulsively reviewed the televised footage of the jets' impact on the World Trade Center lies in part in the feeling of the sublime. Thus Burke:

> The passion caused by the great and sublime in nature ... is Astonishment; and astonishment is that state of the soul, in which all motions are suspended, with some degree of horror. In this case the mind is so entirely filled with its object, that it cannot entertain any other, nor by consequence reason on that object which employs it.
>
> (1990: 53)

In Lyotard's terms, the feeling of astonishment testifies to the existence of a *differend*: with 9/11 'something happens' that remains to be determined. Yet far from regarding this as an opportunity to search for new ways of describing the global hegemony of the West, the response was to call instead for a 'war on terror'. In one sense, again with a glance towards Burke, we might interpret this as a desire to do away with the terror of privation, in this case the privation of reason induced by 'astonishment'. Still again, this time with Lyotard in mind, we might regard this war as motivated by 'nostalgia' for 'the whole and the one, for the reconciliation of the concept and the sensible' (Lyotard 1984: 81–2), in this case by supplying the event with a determinate cause: terrorism. The problem, of course, is that here an indeterminate judgement is being treated as if it were determinate, with the inevitable result of an increase in terror. Rather than testifying to the gulf between reason and experience, the events of 9/11 resulted in calls for their synthesis, with catastrophic results. And this, to adopt Lyotard, is what a politics of the sublime looks like.

CONCLUSIONS

In a radical revision of Kant, Jacques Derrida insists that we regard the sublime as a textual supplement, belonging to the realms of neither pure nor practical reason. As *parergon* to the *ergon* of the *Critique of Judgement*, the sublime gestures towards the lack or contradiction on which the entire Kantian system of thought is founded. Henceforth, any attempt to recover the transcendental dimensions of the sublime must be treated with extreme scepticism. Lyotard, although broadly sympathetic to Kant, similarly discredits the idealist emphasis on the reconciliation of noumena and phenomena. For Lyotard, the sublime is conceived as a disruptive event, forcing critical thought to a crisis. The value of the sublime consists, therefore, precisely in its resistance to rationalist appropriation. Whether demonstrated in the postmodern aesthetics of Newman, or in the refusal of the signs of history to succumb to narrative representation, the resistance of the sublime is ultimately political.

In these postmodern approaches to the sublime, much turns on the relations between the material and the immaterial. For Lyotard, the status of a sublime 'Thing' (1991: 142) is determined again by its resistance to 'mind': '[The sublime thing] is presence as unpresentable to the mind, always withdrawn from its grasp. It does not offer itself to dialogue and dialectic' (142). Lyotard, however, fails to offer a detailed explanation of the status of this sublime thing. What, precisely, renders an object sublime? And what bearing does this have on the nature and significance of the mind? To answer these questions, we must turn to the work of the French psychoanalytical thinker Jacques Lacan and to the critical theorist Slavoj Žižek.

7

FROM THE SUBLIME TO THE RIDICULOUS

LACAN AND ŽIŽEK

From the prohibition of the graven image to Lyotard's stress on the 'sign of history', the sublime has always, in some way, wavered in its relation with the material. While the efforts of poststructuralism have been directed towards reducing the sublime to an effect of language, a number of post-Freudian critics, including Ronald Paulson, David Weiskel, Harold Bloom, and Neil Hertz, have attempted to refigure the sublime in psychological terms, despite Kant's comments on the limitations of this approach (1987: 139). And in a related move, critics such as Christine Battersby, Patricia Yaeger, and Barbara Freeman, observing the gendered nature of the sublime, have approached the concept from a feminist perspective. But whether feminist, psychoanalytic, or deconstructive, what is common to each approach is the desire to trace the transcendental dimensions of the sublime to the effect of some 'thing'. In the wake of these materialist assaults on the sublime, the return to a religious experience of the sublime would appear nonsensical.

In the analysis that follows I want to look in detail at the French psychoanalyst Jacques Lacan's contribution to this debate. It is usual to link Lacanian thought with the materialist tradition outlined above. However, as we shall see, Lacan's relations with philosophical materialism and indeed with the discourse of religion are by no means simple and there may even be a case for regarding Lacanian psychoanalysis as a form of negative theology. As Lacan suggests throughout his teaching, that which is 'nonsensical', including the discourse of religion, may well make sense when judged from the perspective of the sublime. Let us turn now to consider his distinct variations on this theme.

LACAN: SUBLIMITY AND SUBLIMATION

The word 'variations' is appropriate here because, rather disappointingly, Lacan does not get round to presenting a fully elaborated analysis of the sublime. Despite his interest in the excessive and the unbounded, pursued through detailed engagement with Freud, Kant, and other thinkers of the beyond, Lacan seems purposefully to fall short of this task. Twice in his seminar *The Ethics of Psychoanalysis* (1986), for instance, Lacan notes the centrality of the sublime in connection with his thought. In the first case, however, he leaves the task of explaining the concept to another speaker, whose discourse is not printed in the proceedings of the seminar (1992: 286), and in the second his promise to 'take up the question' of 'the Kantian definition of the sublime' is left suspended (301). On what grounds, therefore, should we approach Lacan as a thinker of the sublime?

To answer this question we must consider the basic principles of Jacques Lacan's thought. Working in France from the 1930s to the late 1970s, Lacan became the torchbearer for a radical new approach to Freudian psychoanalysis. Taking the notion of 'the talking cure' at its most literal, he became interested in how subjectivity could be construed as an effect of rather than as a cause of language. Well before Derrida, de Man, and Lyotard proclaimed the idea that the human subject was an arbitrary construct, with no underlying essence or extra-linguistic identity, Lacan set out the ground rules for this new approach to the problem of identity. Drawing on the insights of the Swiss linguist Ferdinand de Saussure, Lacan argued that the unconscious was 'structured like a language' (see Lacan 1979: 20–3). The signifier 'I', for instance, is no more privileged than any other signifier, in so far as its connection with the signified, the concept of identity, is not natural but arbitrary. Thus when I proclaim 'I think therefore I am', I do not affirm my identity; rather the statement indicates a split between the 'I' that speaks (of him- or herself) and the 'I' that is its 'object'.

In Lacan's frequently anthologised paper on 'The Mirror Stage' (1949; see Lacan 1985) he goes on to formulate an account of human subjectivity based on this split. His argument is derived from research into the behaviour of infants of 6–18 months confronted by their image in a mirror. Lacan notes that when gazing in the mirror, the infant experiences two contradictory responses: on the one hand, it experiences joy as it 'recognizes' itself with a 'flutter of jubilant activity'; while, on the other, it feels disappointment when it discovers that this image, 'which offers the promise of wholeness and (self-)identity, is in fact a mirage, a mere reflecting surface which disguises the fragmentation of the infant's felt experience' (Parkin-Gounelas 2001: 6). For Lacan, the realization that the 'ideal I' is unattainable continues to haunt the individual throughout his or her life. Just as in language, the 'I' who speaks and the 'I' that is spoken of fail to coincide, so in the mirror stage we cannot both 'see', as subjective experience, and 'be seen', as object. 'There is a fundamental gap or disjunction between these two operations' (Parkin-Gounelas 2001: 6).

Lacan's therapeutic practice is centred on getting the individual to come to terms with his or her alienated identity, the fact that his or her desire for wholeness or completion is an illusion. Patients who have failed to accept the split in their identity remain in thrall to a state of being known as the Imaginary. They remain convinced that union with the idealized mirror image is possible because they refuse to accommodate themselves to the fact that their identity is an effect of language. Lacan groups the linguistic and social structures, which pre-exist the subject's entry into the world, under the collective term Symbolic. The Symbolic, which the infant normally enters around the age of 2, fulfils two functions. On the one hand, it enables the infant to become a fully-fledged subject; it is able now to articulate and reflect on its needs and desires. On the other hand, the infant is forced to exchange its sense of wholeness for a level of being that is, by virtue of its inscription in language and society, forever compromised by its relation with the desire of the Other.

Entry into the Symbolic comes, therefore, at a price: we give up our fantasies of completion in order to be in the world of words, but the world of words, we soon discover, fails to satisfy. As soon as we enter the symbolic contract, when we learn, for example, that the word 'mother' is no substitute for the real thing, our desire for the lost object, in this case the mother, is born. It is important to grasp at this point that for Lacan the lost object or 'real thing' is essentially missed or missing (see

Lacan 1979: 54–5). That is, the lost object could never be possessed in the first place; as an indicator of the Real, a concept that must be distinguished from empirical reality and, for that matter, from the abstracted reality of the supersensible, the lost object can never be represented. It appears, rather, as the indicator of the central impossibility, the void or 'Thing' at the heart of the Symbolic which can never be presented in reality but which must nevertheless be presupposed if reality is to cohere (Lacan 1992: 119–21).

It is at this point that Lacan begins to engage with the dynamics of the sublime. Although so far in this book we have encountered numerous claims to the effect that the sublime is a product of language, we have yet to look in detail at the arguments underlying these claims. Lacan's thoughts on the relations between language and sublimity are best approached via two commentaries from *The Ethics of Psychoanalysis* (1959–60), the first an interpretation of a therapeutic case study and the second a reading of Sophocles' play *Antigone* (442–441 BCE). The case study, which Lacan encounters in a paper by the analyst Melanie Klein, concerns a woman suffering from depression. This woman, notes Lacan, 'always complained of what she called an empty space inside her, a space she could never fill' (1992: 116). The walls of the woman's house are covered with paintings by her brother-in-law. Eventually the brother-in-law sells one of his paintings, which he removes from the wall and takes away, leaving an empty space. The empty space takes on significance for the woman; it is associated with her own feelings of emptiness. One day, in an attempt to overcome her depression, she starts to 'daub a little' on the wall, so as to 'fill up' the space (116). The woman shows remarkable skill as an artist, so much so that when the painting, or 'thing', is shown to her brother-in-law he proclaims, 'You will never make me believe that it is you who painted that.' What is it that accounts for this miraculous transformation? For Klein, the answer resides in the painting's subject matter: a sequence of images of femininity, culminating 'with the reemergence into the light of day of the image of her own mother at the height of her beauty' (117). It is the lost body of the mother, in other words, that the woman rediscovers in her efforts to fill the vacant space.

Although intrigued by Klein's account, Lacan remains sceptical, arguing that the woman's recovery is not founded on her recovery of the mother but rather realised through the act of 'raising' the mother 'to the dignity of the Thing' (1992: 112). The Thing, let us recall, is the emptiness at the centre of the Real without which signification could not occur. As Lacan puts it, 'the fashioning of the signifier and the introduction of a gap or a hole in the real is identical' (121). In a related formulation the Thing becomes 'that which in the real suffers from the signifier' (118); it exists, in other words, to enable the generation of meaning yet prevents meaning from ever being complete. As such, the Thing has an ambiguous status in the Lacanian schema. Like the Real, the Thing cannot be presented yet must be presupposed. The Thing is therefore 'characterized by the fact that it is impossible for us to imagine it' (125). Like Lyotard's comments on the status of sublime matter, cited in the previous chapter, the Thing for Lacan is a kind of nonthing; we become aware of it as a kind of void or absence residing at the heart of signification.

An object, such as the mother, 'raised to the dignity of the Thing' thus becomes sublime. Lacan, however, at this stage in his argument, refers not to the discourse of sublimity but to the concept of sublimation. As advanced by Freud, sublimation refers to the process by which the libido is transferred from a material object (say, the body of the beloved) towards an object that has no obvious connection with this need (towards, say, the love of God). In Lacan's reworking of Freud this process is reversed: the libido is shifted 'from the void of the "unserviceable" Thing to some concrete, material object of need that assumes a sublime quality the moment it occupies the place of the Thing' (Žižek 1999: 157). The mother is not inherently sublime; rather she becomes sublime because she indicates the void at the heart of symbolization.

The sublime object points, therefore, to the fundamental emptiness, 'the-beyond-of-the-signified' (Lacan 1992: 54) without which no signification could occur. Objects that come to signify this beyond thus become infinitely attractive, fearful, overbearing, or more simply sublime. At this point, Lacan recalls Freud's definitive work *Beyond the Pleasure Principle* (1922), in which Freud argues that psychic life is governed by the desire to regulate pleasure and pain. Too much pleasure, Freud claims, leads to the termination of desire, and thus to the end of life itself. As Lacan summarizes, what Freud calls 'the pleasure principle governs the search for [the lost] object and imposes the detours which maintain the distance in relation to its end' (1992: 58). It is the pleasure principle, in other words, that enables the subject to circle around the void, substituting the illusory satisfaction of the signifier for the deadly encounter with the Thing.

Lacan's discourse on the sublime is picked up later in *The Ethics of Psychoanalysis* in his detailed reading of *Antigone*. The significance of the play turns on the conflict between two value systems: the values of the political system, espoused by the Theban leader, Creon, and the values of familial love, manifested in the devotion of Antigone to her dead and disgraced brother, Polynices. Tragedy is born out of Antigone's refusal to observe Creon's injunction against the extension of burial rites to traitors. Love, she argues, must transcend the good of the state. Rather than speculating, as previous commentators have done, on the rights or wrongs of Antigone's defiance, Lacan focuses instead on Antigone's aesthetic qualities. Antigone, he notes, possesses 'unbearable splendour. She has a quality that both attracts us and startles us, in the sense of intimidates us; this terrible, self-willed victim disturbs us' (247). Such is the splendour of Antigone that she makes any rational consideration of her defiance all but impossible. To the Chorus she thus comes to embody the spirit of Eros, or Love:

> Where is the equal of Love
> ... he is here
> In the bloom of a fair face
> Lying in wait;
> And the grip of his madness
> Spares not god or man,
>
> Marring the righteous man,
> Driving his soul into mazes of sin
> And strife, dividing a house.
> For the light that burns in the eyes of a bride of desire
> Is a life that consumes.
> At the side of the great gods
> Aphrodite immortal
> Works her will upon all.
>
> (lines 780–96; Sophocles 1947)

Antigone, Lacan comments, 'causes the Chorus to lose its head ... [she] makes the just appear unjust, and makes the Chorus transgress all limits, including casting aside any respect it might have for the edicts of the city'. Though Lacan does not refer to Antigone as sublime, her 'beauty' is clearly sublime in effect, causing 'all critical judgements to vacillate, stop[ping] analysis, and plung[ing] the different forms involved into a certain confusion or, rather, an essential blindness' (281). But though Antigone blinds us to reason, she nevertheless reveals the dependence of reason on the forbidden dimensions of the Real. From a Lacanian point of view, Antigone is valued for her refusal to sublimate her desire, to exchange, that is, the object of a forbidden love, her incestuous love for Polynices, for the 'higher' love of the state. As such, she goes to the limit, insisting on the 'unique value' of her brother prior to the imposition of language, culture, and morality (279). The limit, as conceived by Lacan, is 'fatal' since it marks the end of signification, of the substitution of one thing for another, and thus of desire itself. In effect, by failing to submit to the letter of the law, Antigone goes beyond the pleasure principle, and so pursues the object of her desire to the bitter end. As she states at the beginning: 'I am dead and I desire death' (281). What Antigone embraces, therefore, in her desire for Polynices is nothing less than the 'real thing', the deadly object that must be excluded for the rationalization of good and evil to cohere. Antigone, by standing in the place of this deadly thing, thus becomes sublime.

ŽIŽEK

THE SUBLIME OBJECT OF IDEOLOGY

The detailed analysis of the sublime, promised by Lacan but never quite realised, is taken up in the work of the neo-Lacanian theorist, cultural critic, and political philosopher Slavoj Žižek. In this section we will focus on Žižek's most widely known book, *The Sublime Object of Ideology* (1989). As the title indicates, ideology is for Žižek an aesthetic matter. But where Terry Eagleton, in *The Ideology of the Aesthetic* (1990), focuses attention on the concept of the beautiful, by arguing that ideology, like the object of beauty, 'serves to present us with a harmonious whole in which all dissonances have been cancelled' (see Sharpe 2002: 2), Žižek insists that the notion of the 'whole' is unthinkable without reference to the disturbing power of the sublime. The harmony of the *sensus communis* is structured, that is, around an indigestible, irrational core, a sublime Idea that can never occur in reality but which must be presupposed if reality is to cohere (see Myers 2003: 16–17). Just as, in the discourse of the subject, entry into the realm of symbolization is brought about through the foreclosure of the Real, so in the realm of ideology, the integrity of the *sensus communis* is attained, albeit precariously, through the exclusion of a fantasy object. As the critic Matthew Sharpe comments, these 'objects will typically be the presupposed referents of such "master signifiers" as "God", or "the People", or – differently – "the Jews", or "the Bourgeois"' (2002: 2). Because these 'master signifiers' necessarily exceed the ability of political discourse to bring about their realisation, the unification of the subject's experience is never more than provisional. Society, as it were, is based on the subject's (mis)recognition of his/her relation with the unattainable master signifier or Other.

The key to undoing ideology consists, therefore, in locating the underlying impossibility, the unattainable 'enjoyment', of the Other that the sublime object endeavours to conceal (Žižek 1989: 45–9). One way in which ideologies strive to regulate their relation with this fundamental impossibility is through the creation of scapegoats. In the case of Fascism, the figure of 'the Jew' thus becomes the material embodiment of Fascism's failure to achieve its full potential. What 'the Jew' conceals of course is the fact that Fascism is prevented from attaining ideological totality by 'its own antagonistic nature, by its own immanent blockage'. The figure of 'the Jew', as Žižek comments, is thus best understood as a 'paranoid construction', born out of Fascism's failure to come to terms with its inherent lack (127).

The sublime, therefore, as presented by Žižek, ought not to be conceived as a transcendent 'Thing-in-itself' beyond the field of representation, but rather as an indicator of the traumatic emptiness, the primordial lack, residing at the heart of all forms of symbolization. Žižek gathers support for his thesis by turning to the work of the German philosopher G. W. F. Hegel (1770–1831), whose critique of the Kantian sublime, presented explicitly in the *Aesthetics* (1832–40; 1975: I, 362–3) and implicitly in the *Phenomenology of Spirit* (1807; 1977: §§

343–5), is directed precisely at the false distinction between the sensible and the supersensible. As Žižek emphasises, in Kant's system the gap between the empirical and the transcendental 'is abolished in a negative way', for even 'if the Ideas of reason can be in no way adequately presented [in the sensuous, empirical world], they can be revived and evoked in the mind by means of this very inadequacy which can be presented in a sensuous way' (1989: 203). According to Žižek, where Hegel differs from Kant is in his insistence that the failure of the empirical to present the transcendental 'Thing-in-itself' indicates that 'this Thing-in-itself is nothing but this [experience] of radical negativity' (205–6). For Hegel, in short, the sublime is 'an object whose positive body is just an embodiment of Nothing' (206).

We are now in a position to offer a more exacting definition of the sublime object. Where in Kant the feeling of the sublime is evoked by the awe-inspiring and the boundless, in, say, the infinite grandeur of the mountain or the raging of the sea, in Hegel the emphasis falls on the 'incompatible' and the 'incomparable'. The mountain, that is, does not point to the existence of a supersensible realm, beyond appearance, but rather to the inadequacy of appearance to itself, to the sense in which appearance, or phenomena, is orientated around a determinate lack. Again, Žižek stresses, with a glance to Lacan, that the sublime object is merely the embodiment of this lack. As such, it is more appropriate to conceive of the sublime in contradictory formulations such as 'the Spirit *is* the Bone', 'the State *is* the Monarch', or 'God *is* Christ' (207; see Hegel 1977: §§ 343–5). In either case, there is an Idea, of the State or of the divine, only in so far as there is some thing, the contingent body of the Monarch, or the suffering, finite body of Jesus, that prevents the Idea from achieving its full ontological identity. To this end, the transcendent Idea and its materialisation (the object that embodies the lack that *is* the Idea) are strictly correlative: there is an Idea only in so far as there is some material thing, a surplus object in which, precisely, the Idea cannot be fully presented. To return to the example cited above: the inability of Fascism to present itself as a totality is materialised in the figure of 'the Jew'. Having failed to attain the unity of phenomena and Idea, a unity corresponding in aesthetic terms to the category of the beautiful, 'the Jew' is presented to the German people as literally surplus to requirements. Simultaneously fascinating and repulsive, the hideous sublimity of 'the Jew' signifies the inability of Fascism to be anything other than a fractured or empty totality.

Might a similar logic be applied to the efforts of the Bush regime in America to comprehend the tragedy of 11 September 2001 and its brutal aftermath? As Žižek observes in *Welcome to the Desert of the Real* (2002), the ideological deployment of the signifier 'evil', in connection with the three nations Iran, Iraq, and North Korea, is the means by which America and its allies deflect attention from their own internal antagonisms. The 'axis of evil', and associated bodies such as the literally ungraspable Osama Bin Laden and the shadowy Al Qaida, thus become sublime objects of ideology. In so far as they exceed the comprehension of America, these objects embody the nation's failure both to come to terms with the trauma of 9/11 and to conceal, or 'foreclose', the internal contradictions which contributed to this trauma.

How, then, should we account for the current crisis? Is it enough to say that a sublime event, such as 9/11, is 'a product' of the inherent failure of symbolisation, of the inability of the capitalist West to be anything other than fractured or lacking? Throughout his writing, Žižek is careful to avoid reducing the relationship between the symbolic and the sublime to one of cause and effect, at least not in any straightforward sense. Rather, as he points out in *The Fragile Absolute*, the relationship between the two is 'indeterminable' (2000a: 92). Thus, whilst in one sense, the destruction of the Twin Towers appears as the disruptive, overwhelming event that brings about the new symbolic world regime, which in turn renders this event retroactively 'unspeakable', in another sense one can also claim the exact opposite: is not the mythical status of 9/11 itself a fantasy-formation, brought about by the West as a means of concealing the founding gap, or void, that prevents it from attaining ideological consistency? In simpler terms, we are at a loss to decide which comes first: the symbolic structure or the violent, disruptive event. The sublime ought, therefore, to be seen not as a founding myth, generated by the symbolic, but rather as that which must be *excluded* so that the symbolic order can maintain its consistency (96). It is more accurate to say that the creation of the empty or 'sacred' place of the Thing is strictly correlative to the creation of the errant object marking the place of this Thing. The raising of the good sublime object, whether conceived as 'America' or 'freedom', is thus linked reflexively with the bad sublime object, posited as 'evil', 'terror', or 'Al Qaida'. As Žižek argues, such objects 'are not two different entities, but the obverse and reverse of one and the same entity' (27). A related argument is set out by the postmodern philosopher Jean Baudrillard in his essay *The Spirit of Terrorism* (2002; see also Baudrillard 2005). For Baudrillard, the distinction between terrorist evil and Western good is the product of a mutually reinforcing binary opposition, 'in which it is impossible to conceive of one pole without also bringing the other into conceptual existence' (Hawkes 2003: 188). Like Žižek, Baudrillard regards the dominance of such binary oppositions as the underlying cause of ideological conflict. Where Žižek advances on Baudrillard, however, is in highlighting the extent to which the division of the world into good and bad sublime objects may be overcome through an act of analytical self-recognition. Though not overly positive in his assessment of this act as a practical reality, Žižek nevertheless points to a route beyond the totalitarian politics of the sublime.

THE ART OF THE RIDICULOUS SUBLIME

Žižek's analysis of the sublime is not restricted to the realms of politics and ideology; inevitably, given the origins of the concept in the discourse of aesthetics, his work also embraces readings of literature, film, music, and painting. In simple terms, Žižek maintains that a work of art, like a political 'system', is bound up in a reflexive relation with a repressed object of desire. The work of art is thus enabled and, at the same time, endangered by its fascination with that which is foreclosed, repressed, or more simply sublime. Žižek's commentaries on works of art are numerous, and range from revealing insights into modernist literature, opera, and other instances of 'high art' to detailed readings of popular fiction, advertising, and *film noir*. In a few moments we will consider how this analysis leads to a provocative commentary on the representation of woman; but for now, so that we may get a sense of how Žižekian cultural criticism works, let us return to a previously cited example: the abstract painting of Barnett Newman.

For Lyotard, the vertical line or 'zip' in a painting such as *Adam* (1951–2) signifies the primary act of creation, dividing an otherwise undifferentiated plane in order to stimulate the emergence of 'the event'. But what exactly is the zip and how exactly does it perform this role? Though Žižek does not conduct a reading of Newman, it might be useful to regard the zip as a form of 'master signifier': 'a signifier of nothing other than of signifying as such'. *Adam* thus becomes an illustration of the Lacanian idea that 'the fashioning of the signifier and the introduction of a gap or a hole in the real is identical' (Lacan 1992: 120–1). There is, in other words, an effect of the sublime only in so far as there is some material limit, in this case a zip, that resists sublimation (see Žižek 2000a: 29).

In what amounts to a more precise analysis than Lyotard's, we may now account for the viewer's desire for the sublime encounter in terms of the relation between the object and the Thing. As the gap in the real, the sacred Thing is never presented as such, but only retroactively after it has been disturbed by the appearance of a material object. The object itself is unimportant, and indeed much contemporary art plays on the idea that anything, even excrement, can serve as an indicator of the sublime. As Žižek observes, contemporary art is painfully aware that the distinction between the sublime and the ridiculous is a matter of degree. The problem is that today, 'in the double movement of progressive commodification of aesthetics and the aestheticification of the universe of commodities', an aesthetically 'pleasing' object is less and less able to sustain the role of the material limit necessary for the raising of the sublime. Paradoxically, what today's artists strive to achieve through the exhibition of excremental objects in the 'sacred' space of the art gallery is confirmation that the radical incongruity between object and Thing still applies. As Žižek concludes, today's artists, 'far from undermining the logic of sublimation, are desperately trying to *save* it ... without the minimal gap between [the object] and the [empty place of the Thing], there simply is no symbolic order' (2000: 32).

Therefore, rather than talking of an opposition between the sublime and the ridiculous, it makes more sense to speak of their co-implication. In *The Art of the Ridiculous Sublime* (2000b), Žižek pursues this idea through a detailed reading of David Lynch's neo *film noir*, *Lost Highway* (1997). The central character of Lynch's film is literally divided in two: in the first half the apparently impotent Fred is imprisoned for the murder of his apparently adulterous wife Renee; in the second half, Fred is transformed into another person entirely. As the younger, virile Pete,

Fred becomes involved with the sexually voracious Alice, herself a blond reincarnation of Renee. Following a passionate sex scene in a desert motel, after whispering into Pete's ear 'You'll never have me!' Alice disappears into a wooden house, which promptly goes up in flames. At this point, her violent mobster lover Mr Eddy, the man responsible for luring her into a life of prostitution and pornography, turns up on the scene. A conflict follows with Pete, who is now transformed back into Fred, culminating in the execution of Mr Eddy by a 'Mystery Man', the same man who warned Fred, in the film's first half, of his wife's transgressions.

Two points emerge from Žižek's reading of the film. The first concerns Mr Eddy, an obscene father figure who seems to embody both the sublime and the ridiculous. The former is played out through an excessive regard for 'the rules'. As Žižek comments, Mr Eddy, by pushing respect for the law to the point of absurdity, reveals how the sublime logic of the Law, in the Kantian sense (see chapter 4), is asserted only on the basis of some ridiculously contingent, arbitrary act of will. Like other larger-than-life characters in Lynch's universe, such as Frank in *Blue Velvet* (1986) or Bobby Peru in *Wild at Heart* (1990), Mr Eddy's obsession with the sublime is focussed on and facilitated by a hearty engagement with the ordinary. In effect, it is precisely through their hyperactive enjoyment of the everyday that such characters highlight the minimal gap separating reality from the Real.

The second point is derived from Lynch's complicated representation of female sexuality. As we have seen, theories of the sublime have traditionally linked the feminine with ideas of the beautiful and the masculine with ideas of the sublime. Most notoriously, in Burke and Kant, the sublime is associated with deep, or male, understanding, and the beautiful with shallow, or female, understanding. Recent feminist readings of the sublime have endeavoured to challenge this reading, either by stressing the subversive or aberrant effects of representations of femininity in male-authored texts or by uncovering evidence of a feminine sublime in texts written by women. Žižek's contribution to this debate, based on his reading of Lacan's theorisation of feminine sexuality, is of course highly provocative. In simple terms *Lost Highway* divides femininity in half, leaving, on the one side, the impassive, withdrawn, and ultimately unavailable woman represented by Renee, and, on the other, the sexually aggressive, outspoken, and all too available Alice. The first woman is murdered for her unavailability and the second woman, arguably conjured up by Fred/Pete as a form of psychic compensation, disappears as a result of her impossibility: 'You'll never have me!' a statement that precipitates the transformation of the virile Pete back into the impotent Fred. Both images of femininity thus conform to the Lacanian thesis of woman as the foreclosed or sublime object of patriarchal discourse, a thesis warranting the oft-cited and much misunderstood assertion that woman, as such, does not exist. What this means is that woman, unlike man, is liberated from the constraints of the signifier. Like Antigone, she becomes sublime on account of her ability to enjoy bliss, or *jouissance*, beyond the limits of symbolization. When the sublime dimensions of the feminine are encountered in the masculine universe, masculine identity begins to break down.

TOWARDS THE FRAGILE ABSOLUTE

The depiction of the ungraspable woman in *Lost Highway* indicates the fundamental deadlock of the sexual relationship: the idea that the beloved can never be incorporated in the subject's symbolic universe and that all attempts to rectify this deadlock, through murder or fantasy, must end in failure. No amount of sublimation can alter the fact that woman, as object, is sublime only on account of her ability to occupy the place of the sacred Thing. Since the lover, in the famous Lacanian formulation, desires that which in the beloved is more than the beloved (see Lacan 1979: 268), his attempt to possess this elusive quality is doomed to fail. Indeed it seems that the only possibility of oneness with the beloved is attained in death. To reiterate in terms of the sublime: *ekstasis* is achieved only at the moment when the subject exceeds the limits of symbolization. Thus, to return to the case of Antigone, the tragic heroine realises her desire but only on condition that she renounce her relation with the Symbolic. The price she must pay for encountering the Real of her desire is her own death.

As Lacan's analysis of *Antigone* illustrates, love is central to the discourse of the sublime. But it is in religious discourse that the relations between love, sublimation, and the ungraspable dimensions of the Other, in this case God, become especially marked. Let us recall that signification begins with the creation of a void or hollow in the Real. In Lacan's words, 'what man demands, what he cannot help but demand, is to be deprived of something real' (1992: 150). Man's desire for the Other is the result of this primary deprivation. The emptiness at the heart of the Real, which desire endeavours to capture, is of course the Thing. As the example of courtly love shows, the love object becomes sublime on account of its elevation to the inaccessible place of the Thing. The problem with courtly love, however, is that the sublimation of the woman does not necessarily make her status as a 'sexual object' disappear – 'far from it; the sexual object as such may come to light in sublimation' (Lacan 1992: 161). Thus Lacan cites the example of a satirical troubadour poem by Arnaud Daniel in which 'the idealized woman' commands 'her knight to put his mouth to her trumpet' or vagina, an order designed to test the worthiness of his love. As Lacan comments:

> the Lady, who is in the position of the Other and of the object, finds herself suddenly and brutally positing, in a place knowingly constructed out of the most refined of signifiers, the emptiness of a thing in all its crudity, a thing that reveals itself in its nudity to be the thing, her thing, the one that is to be found at her very heart in its cruel emptiness. That Thing ... is in a way unveiled with a cruel and insistent power.

> (163)

As soon as the woman is encountered in her substance, she changes from the sacred object to the transgressive abject (see Kristeva 1982); she is shown, that is, from the point of view of masculine desire, to be monstrously sublime.

In a related manner, if religious discourses of the sublime are to protect themselves from the return of the monstrous, they must ensure that the fleshly cognates of mortal love are kept at bay. In Paul's second letter to the Corinthians, love is thus redefined as *agape*, a pure transcendental love, freed from all references to *eros*. Since *agape* proceeds without reference to a material object, it may be seen as an attempt to sidestep the logic of sublimation and thus to save the beyond of the sacred. This explains why Paul is keen to distinguish love from knowledge. As he writes in 1 Corinthians 13:

> If I speak in the tongues of mortals and of angels, but do not have love, I am a noisy gong or a clanging cymbal. And if I have prophetic powers, and understand all mysteries and all knowledge, and if I have all faith, as to remove mountains, but do not have love, I am nothing. If I give away all my possessions, and if I hand over my body so that I may boast [alternative translation: to be burned], but do not have love, I gain nothing. ... Love never ends. But as for prophecies, they will come to an end; as for tongues, they will cease; as for knowledge, it will come to an end. For we know only in part, and we prophesy only in part; but when the complete comes, the partial will come to an end. ... For now we see in a mirror, dimly, but then we will see face to face. Now I know only in part; then I will know fully, even as I have been fully known. And now faith, hope, and love abide, these three; and the greatest of these is love.
>
> (Žižek, 2000a: 145–6)

Though knowledge may be 'all', knowledge without love is 'nothing'. But what is love? On the one hand, although love, unlike knowledge, 'never ends', it is clearly only 'now', while I exist as faulty and incomplete, that 'faith, hope, and love abide'. Love, in other words, is available only to a being conceived in relation to lack, a being who loves only because he or she does not know all. Love, as Žižek puts it, is thus 'not an exception to the All of knowledge, but precisely that "nothing" which makes even the complete series/field of knowledge incomplete' (2000a: 146). Love corresponds to the empty, enigmatic dimension of the Thing, the void, or no-thing around which the symbolic order is structured and without which symbolisation could not occur.

Yet as much as *agape* appears to transcend the corporeal, and thus to fulfil the requirements of a sacred sublime, Paul insists that the greatness of love, higher even than absolute knowledge, is available only to a being humbly aware of itself as 'nothing'. The idea of the sacred, that is, is bound in a reflexive relation with an empirical object, in this case the vulnerable, suffering body of Christ. Christ, in other words, is the material remainder, the sacrificial lamb, which embodies the absolute negativity of the divine. Through Christ's sacrifice, Paul maintains in his second letter, the 'veil' dividing humanity from God is 'taken away' (2 Corinthians 3: 16–18). Christ thus becomes sublime in so far as his mortality stands in the place of the overwhelming glory of God.

But in a more startling sense, Paul goes on to suggest that God's glory can only appear if God is incarnated in human form. The primary division in the human subject between lack and plenitude is thus echoed in the holy division between the empirical Son and the transcendental Spirit. If 'the Lord is the Spirit', the 'freedom' of this Spirit is nevertheless bound in a reflexive relationship with the material residue, that is, the inert sacrificial body of Christ. As confirmed by the hideous violence portrayed in Mel Gibson's film *The Passion of the Christ* (2004), the force of Christianity is bound up with its ability to raise an abject object to the status of the Thing. Unlike courtly love, the abject object does not threaten the logic of sublimation but is turned to a principle of its support. It is not Christ's beauty, but rather his abjection and his subsequent transformation into a sublime object of desire that enables his followers to bear the inexhaustible dimensions of the sacred Thing; what St Paul describes, in 2 Corinthians: 3, as the blinding light of God's glory.

CONCLUSIONS

In Žižek's reading of Lacanian psychoanalysis, the sublime is identified, via Hegel, as the 'reified' effect of the inconsistency of the symbolic order. The fascination of the sublime is thus derived from its status as an indicator of the Thing, the emptiness at the heart of the Real without which signification could not occur. Objects are not in themselves sublime, rather they become sublime when they are raised 'to the dignity of the Thing'. The terror of the sublime is brought about through its relation with the Real. In Lacan's theory, the Real is the ultimate contradiction in terms in so far as it both precedes and succeeds the symbolic. As such, the Real is impossible and appears only as the failure or void of the symbolic. Whenever an object is made to represent this void it becomes an object of fascination, provoking love or hatred in accordance with the extent to which the symbolic order is perceived to be in harmony or in crisis. Thus the crucifixion of Christ can be explained as a reaction formation to the perception of the extreme discord, the gap, between God and the lowest form of human existence. It follows that Christ's apotheosis, his transformation into a sublime object of desire, marks the point at which the horror of the void is sublimated as the glory of the Thing.

AFTERWORD

RETURN TO BEAUTY

According to the contemporary French philosopher Jean-Luc Nancy, the sublime forms a

> fashion that has persisted uninterruptedly into our own time from the beginnings of modernity. ... it has always been a fashion because it has always concerned a break within or from aesthetics ... it has been a kind of defiance with which aesthetics provokes itself – 'enough beauty already, we must be sublime!'
>
> (1993: 25)

The sublime, on this account, is the means by which art suspends or disrupts itself 'in view of something other than art' (27). But this movement is not restricted to the sphere of aesthetics. As we have seen, sublimity could be said to mark the point at which thought itself is brought into question. If the beautiful relates to notions of unity and harmony, then the sublime refers to fragmentation and disharmony, to the moment when thought trembles on the edge of extinction. Thus, to give an example, the Enlightenment faith in reason meets its suspension in the Romantic fascination with the numinous. And, in turn, this sense of a transcendent realm, beyond the limits of the empirical world, is challenged by the materialist stress on sublimity as an effect of appearances, as Žižek proposes, or of signification, as de Man and Derrida have argued. In either case, sublimity arises when the harmony of a body of thought is brought into question.

In this sense, we might go on to argue that the category of the sublime is another name for contradiction. Whenever, that is, art encounters the inadequacy of its claim to represent the truth, *then* sublimity arises to push art towards its final destination or *telos*. For Hegel, whose theory of the dialectic underpins this view, the end of art is attained when truth is capable of presenting itself on its own without any recourse to representation. But this mode of pure presentation is achieved only negatively. Truth, for Hegel, cannot appear except as the sublime contradiction of some kind of sensible form (Hegel 1975: I, 363; Žižek 1989: 6). Put more simply, this means that there is no realm of truth independent of finite, formed appearances. And since appearances, as Žižek argues, are always lacking, formed, that is, on the basis of their exclusion of some contradictory, impossible object, otherwise known as the Real, then the truth is no longer a noumenal, freely indeterminate beyond, but rather 'the ultimate emptiness of all our gestures' (Milbank 2004: 228).

Such a conclusion, as the theologian John Milbank observes, is essentially nihilistic, not least because it precludes any possibility of returning to the beautiful. Looked at from another perspective, however, might we not regard the sublime in a positive light as the means by which the beautiful is prevented from slipping into the merely agreeable? As Nancy puts it, when the beautiful is consumed in the agreeable, i.e. when it is identified with personal liking or taste, then 'the beautiful ultimately loses its quality of beauty (for in enjoyment, in the beautiful as satisfied or satisfying, the beautiful is finished – and art along with it)' (1993: 33). The beautiful, that is, only attains its 'proper' quality when it is deranged by the sublime. As Nancy goes on to state, 'the sublime represents ... nothing less than that without which the beautiful could be nothing but the beautiful (which paradoxically comes down to the same thing)' (34). Though the sublime, as Kant insists, is concerned with the unlimited, it ought not to be confused with the infinite. Rather, Nancy continues, 'it is a matter ... of the movement of the unlimited, or more exactly, of the "unlimitation" ... that takes place on the border of the limit, and thus on the border of the presentation' (35). In other words, Nancy appears at first to agree with Žižek that the sublime 'takes place neither in a hidden world withdrawn from our own nor in a world of "Ideas" nor in the world of a "nonrepresentable" something or other' (49). Instead the sublime is conceived as an offering or gesture that takes place at the limit of art. Where Nancy departs from Žižek, however, it is in his refusal to reduce the effect of sublimity to material inertia. As an offering, the sublime is neither identified with the metaphysical beyond, nor is it merely reduced to the sensible present. Rather it functions, simply, as the movement that enables mind to think freely, without reference to determinate concepts. Thus, for Nancy, the sublime is that which enables the beautiful to surpass itself, and so to be open to the possibility of a presentation that is always to come.

It may be, however, that even Nancy's emphasis on the freedom afforded by the sublime fails to do justice to the beautiful. As the literary and cultural critic Elaine Scarry has noted, the juxtaposition of the sublime and the beautiful, a 'fashion' dating back at least to Burke, has had the unfortunate effect of blocking the mind in its ascent from the sensible to the transcendental. Since, as Kant goes on to argue, the supersensible realm is apprehended negatively, only, that is, when imagination fails to supply an Idea with a concept, it becomes impossible to put Ideas, such as truth or justice, into practice (Scarry 2000: 82–6 *passim*). In similar vein, Milbank has argued that the distinction between the sublime and the beautiful is not only false, but also pernicious. During the medieval and Patristic eras, for example, the beautiful was regarded as coterminous with divine truth, and while sublimity, as we noted in Augustine and later in Dante, certainly involved some form of disruption, it was 'yet not a total rupture, since the unlimited was held to be, in its simplicity, an unimaginable infinite fullness of beautiful form, not its negation' (Milbank 2004: 213; see also Crockett 2001). Sublimity, in other words, was regarded as a mode of beauty, not as an exception, and truth was thus available for apprehension by the individual. It is only with the dawn of the Enlightenment that truth is figured as inaccessible and the sublime is reconceived as a category of cognitive failure.

A number of conclusions follow from this observation. Firstly, the privileging of the Kantian or negative sublime severed the unlimited not only from the field of representation, but also from the sphere of practice. Thus, Milbank argues, Kant fails 'to recover the sense that the unknown is not simply that which cannot be represented, but is also that which arrives, which ceaselessly but imperfectly makes itself known again in every new event' (2004: 217). This means the sublime in subjectivity is no longer identified with the actions of an individual but instead with 'the abstract fact of his possession of an indeterminate freedom' (217). Such a freedom is cold, impersonal, and, as we saw in the example from Morrison's *Beloved* (chapter 4), impossible to conceive. In a related sense, if the essence of the true ethical sublime is freedom, a freedom we are to love merely for its own sake, without reference to our own desires, then this runs against the Platonic tradition, with its stress on the continuity of truth, justice, and personal satisfaction. In Platonism and Neoplatonism the beautiful is linked with *eros*, an embodied desire leading naturally to an elevated desire for true intellectual beauty. It is only later in the Western tradition, with the growing influence of Protestantism, that *agape*, the selfless, disinterested form of love, is sundered entirely from *eros*. Milbank concludes that the influence of the Kantian sublime results in a conception of the divine emptied of all positive content. If humans cannot desire their God, then love for such a God is rendered 'cold ... abstract and empty' (219).

What, then, may we say in support of a return to the beautiful? In medieval thought, as we have seen, the beautiful granted form to the ineffable. It enabled humans to mediate the infinite with the finite through its connection with *eros*. In practice, sublimity cannot be separated from the appreciation of form. What attracts us to the sublime is not an abstract quality but the fact that the sense of the awe-inspiring or the overpowering is conveyed in *this* particular mountain, in *this* particular moment. In making this judgement, however, we must be careful to avoid lapsing into neo-Hegelianism. For Hegel, the sublime is revealed in the mountain's appearance but this 'outward shaping is itself annihilated in turn by what it reveals' (1975: I, 363). The particular mountain is again of no importance, and, moreover, that which it is said to reveal, let us say the infinite, proves once again to be inaccessible and unknowable. The Kantian and Hegelian legacy is the same: wanting what it cannot have; the subject of the sublime is locked in melancholia, divorced for ever from the object of its desire.

For Milbank, the key to release from this condition is to admit the persistence of desire. For as soon as *eros*, conceived here as the love of the particular, is added to the sublime it becomes possible, once again, to conceive of the infinite as 'in *analogical continuity* with what lies within' the finite (2004: 229). Though this does not mean, of course, that the infinite can be mastered or possessed, the reintroduction of desire does at least hold out the possibility of engagement. A world of whiteness and 'snowy scents', as the poet Wallace Stevens proposes in 'The Poems of Our Climate', is impossible to conceive, for what humans crave is the warmth of a relationship (Stevens 1984). Our relationship with the beyond is thus offered in trust, like a prayer. Accepting that the forms of this world are incomplete, we offer our own judgements in a related spirit, expecting these to be judged in turn, and in ways that cannot be anticipated. On this basis, no longer terrified by the voiding or loss of the sublime object, we engage in a form of 'delightful longing' (Milbank 2004: 229). 'Where this is denied', as Milbank puts it, 'and the sublime is sundered from the beautiful – eventually, as in postmodern nihilism to the point of obliterating it – then the passage to the sublime leads not to union with a living other, but to a dispassionate freedom which beckons us beyond encounter to total fusion' (230). We are sustained, then, by our desire for the other, an other separated by distance and by difference. Such an other must be conceived, like ourselves, as radically incomplete. And when, in the experience of the sublime, the other is revealed in this way, we need not despair, for on both accounts self and other 'are completed in [their] very incompletion' (231).

GLOSSARY

A priori (Kant):   Knowledge derived from abstract reasoning, prior to experience (see *empiricism* and *idealism* below).

Aesthetics (Kant):   The branch of philosophy concerned with the study of art.

Beauty (Plato, Kant):   Until the eighteenth century, beauty was the main focus of *aesthetics* (see above). According to Plato, beauty was said to inhere within objects. For Kant, beauty is determined by a judgement of *taste* (see below) and is thus more closely linked with the mind. In general, beauty is used of objects and ideas possessing harmony, coherence, integrity, and formal perfection. From the middle of the eighteenth century it was frequently opposed to the *sublime* (see below).

Concept (Kant):   A general or abstract term under which many individual instances of things or events may be classed.

Deconstruction (Derrida, de Bolla, de Man):   A theory and a critical practice which insists that notions of truth and coherence in a text are illusory and that the meaning of a text is always indeterminate.

Dialectics (Hegel, Žižek):   In Hegelian dialectics thought begins with a thesis, or idea, which is then countered by an antithesis, an opposing idea. The conflict is resolved by combining thesis and antithesis in a synthesis, which compromises a greater, more encompassing idea. Thus, the thesis 'all dogs are friendly' is countered by the antithesis 'but this dog is vicious'. The opposing claims are then resolved in the synthesis 'most dogs are friendly'. Žižek opposes the synthesising tendency of Hegel's dialectic, arguing that contradiction, or antithesis, is an essential condition of every thesis. Thus, the claim 'but this dog is vicious' is central to the claim 'all dogs are friendly', for without the existence of the vicious dog we would have no grounds for comparison.

Differend (Lyotard): A conflict that cannot be equitably resolved for lack of a mutually applicable rule of judgement.

Discourse (de Bolla): A mode of speaking, writing, and thinking determined by specific ideological rules and attitudes.

Empiricism (Burke, Locke, Hume): The belief that all knowledge is derived from or based on experience.

Enlightenment (Locke, Hume, Kant): The Enlightenment period emerged in the late seventeenth century and is characterised by a faith in scientific and philosophical progress.

Epistemology (Locke, Hume, Kant): The branch of philosophy concerned with the theory of knowledge.

Idealism (Plato, Kant, Schelling *et al.*): The belief that our sense of reality is determined wholly or in part by the structure of our minds.

Ideology (Marx, Žižek): A systematically false perception of the real conditions of existence.

Imaginary (Lacan): A condition of being prior to the entry into language (see the *Symbolic* below) in which there is no clear distinction between subject and object.

Judgement (Kant): For Kant, judgements of taste in the sphere of *aesthetics* (see above) must be distinguished from judgements about the agreeable. A truly aesthetic judgement is disinterested, i.e. it is a judgement based on reflection rather than on sense. Reflective judgements, such as 'this painting is beautiful', are indeterminate in so far as they proceed without reference to a *concept* (see above). Although 'subjective', the judgement of taste demands universal assent.

Materialism (Marx *et al.*): The belief that whatever exists is either matter or can be reduced to matter. The definition of matter is, however, debatable and extends, in some extreme cases, e.g. *deconstruction* (see above), to the materiality of language.

Metaphysics (Plato, Kant *et al.*):   The branch of philosophy concerned with establishing underlying conditions of knowledge, beyond the realm of sensory experience (see *ontology* below).

Neo-classical (Pope): A cultural movement, originating in the late seventeenth century, which attempts to recover and adhere to the aesthetic ideals of the Augustan period of the Roman empire (c. 63 BCE–14 CE).

Neoplatonism (Plotinus, Shaftesbury):   A school of thought combining Plato's philosophy with elements of *Stoicism* (see below) and Christianity.

Noumena (Kant):   Noumena refers to the underlying conditions of experience, which are not knowable as *things-in-themselves* (see below), but which must be presupposed if our experience of reality or phenomena is to cohere.

Ontology (Plato, Kant):   The branch of *metaphysics* (see above) that considers existence as a *thing-in-itself* (see below), apart from any actual or existing thing.

Parergon (Kant, Derrida):   The Latin word for the frame or border surrounding a building or a work of art.

Platonism (Plato):   The central doctrine of Plato's philosophy is the theory of Forms or Ideas. An Idea, in the Platonic sense, is an eternal, transcendental reality, which may be conceived by the mind without reference to sense experience. Platonic Ideas such as the beautiful and the true function as a form of universal standard or model for instances of the beautiful and the true in the empirical world.

Postmodernism   (Baudrillard,   Derrida,   Jameson,   Lyotard, Žižek):   A late twentieth-century/early twenty-first-century cultural movement. Defining characteristics of postmodernism include: a sceptical attitude (see *Scepticism* below) towards fixed ideas of truth, morality, and reason; rejection of the Enlightenment (see above) ideal of human 'progress'; a focus on the socially, politically, and linguistically determined 'subject' (see *subjectivity* below), as opposed to the autonomous, integrated 'self'.

Rationalism (Descartes, Kant): The philosophical belief in reason as the foundation of all knowledge.

Real (Lacan): As opposed to reality, which constitutes our everyday experience of being in the world, the Real stands for that which is neither *Imaginary* (see above) nor *Symbolic* (see below). As the missing or foreclosed element of the *Symbolic*, the Real may be gestured towards but never grasped, hence the claim that the Real is missing, or impossible (see also *Thing* below).

Scepticism (Hume): The belief that true and objective knowledge of existence is impossible (see also *postmodernism* above).

Stoicism (Philo Judaeus, Shaftesbury): Ancient Greek philosophy combining elements of *empiricism* and *materialism* (see above), and later with *Neoplatonism* (see above) and Christianity. Stoicism maintains that human reason is an aspect of cosmic or universal reason, otherwise known as nature. To live virtuously, according to Stoic ethics, is to live in accordance with nature.

Subjectivity (de Bolla, Derrida, Lacan *et al.*): The term used to describe the sense in which human identity is subjected to or determined by a range of political, historical, social, and linguistic forces.

Sublime (Longinus, Burke, Kant *et al.*): The highest of the high; that which is without comparison; the awe-inspiring or overpowering; the unbounded and the undetermined (see *beauty* above).

Symbolic (Lacan): The symbolic order refers to the realm of signification or language that determines the emergence and condition of the subject (see *subjectivity* and the *Imaginary* and the *Real* above).

Thing (Lacan): the enigmatic void or emptiness at the heart of the real brought about through the intervention of the symbolic order.

Thing-in-itself (Kant): that which exists independently of experience.

BIBLIOGRAPHY

Abrams, M. H. (1971) *Natural Supernaturalism: Tradition and Revolution in Romantic Literature*, New York: W. W. Norton and Company.

Ashfield, A. and de Bolla, P. (eds) (1996) *The Sublime: A Reader in Eighteenth-Century Aesthetic Theory*, Cambridge: Cambridge University Press.

Auerbach, E. (1965) *Literary Language and Its Public in Late Latin Antiquity and in the Middle Ages*, trans. Ralph Manheim, London: Routledge and Kegan Paul.

Baillie, J. (1953) *An Essay on the Sublime* with an Introduction by Samuel Holt Monk, The Augustan Reprint Society 43, Los Angeles: University of California Press.

Battersby, C. (1989) *Gender and Genius: Towards a Feminist Aesthetics*, London: Women's Press.

Baudrillard, J. (2002) *The Spirit of Terrorism*, trans. Chris Turner, London: Verso.

—— *The Intelligence of Evil, or the Lucidity Pact*, trans. Chris Turner, Oxford: Berg.

Bennington, G. and Derrida, J. (1993) *Jacques Derrida*, trans. Geoffrey Bennington, Chicago and London: University of Chicago Press.

Bernstein, J. M. (1992) *The Fate of Art: Aesthetic Alienation from Kant to Derrida and Adorno*, Cambridge: Polity Press.

Bloom, H. (1973) *The Anxiety of Influence: A Theory of Poetry*, Oxford: Oxford University Press.

Brody, J. (1958) *Boileau and Longinus*, Geneva: Librairie E. Droz.

Brown, D.B. and Young, D. (2004) *Mariele Neudecker: Over and Over, Again and Again*, London: Tate St Ives.

Burke, E. (1958–78) *The Correspondence of Edmund Burke*, 10 vols, ed. Thomas W. Copeland, Cambridge: Cambridge University Press.

—— (1969) *Reflections on the Revolution in France and on the Proceedings in Certain Societies in London Relative to that Event*, ed. Conor Cruise O'Brien, Harmondsworth: Penguin.

—— (1990) *A Philosophical Enquiry into the Origin of Our Ideas of the*

Sublime and the Beautiful, ed. Adam Phillips, Oxford: Oxford
University Press.

Burnet, J. (1965) The Sacred Theory of the Earth, ed. Basil Wiley, London:
Centaur Press.

Burnham, D. (2000) An Introduction to Kant's Critique of Judgement,
Edinburgh: Edinburgh University Press.

Cheetham, M. (2001) Kant, Art, and Art History: Moments of Discipline,
Cambridge: Cambridge University Press.

Cole, L. and Swartz, R. G. (1994) ' "Why Should I Wish for Words?":
Literacy, Articulation, and the Borders of Literary Culture', in At the
Limits of Romanticism: Essays in Cultural, Feminist, and Materialist
Criticism, ed. Mary A. Favret and Nicola J. Watson, Bloomington
and Indianapolis: Indiana University Press.

Coleridge, S. T, (1956–71) Collected Letters of Samuel Taylor Coleridge, 6
vols, ed. E. L. Griggs, Oxford: Oxford University Press.

—— (1957–90) The Notebooks of Samuel Taylor Coleridge, 4 vols, ed.
Kathleen Coburn, The Collected Works of Samuel Taylor Coleridge,
Bollingen Series, London and Princeton, NJ: Princeton University
Press.

—— (1972) Lay Sermons, ed. R. J. White, The Collected Works of Samuel
Taylor Coleridge, Bollingen Series, London and Princeton, NJ:
Princeton University Press.

—— (1995) Shorter Works and Fragments, ed. H. J. Jackson and J. R. de J.
Jackson, The Collected Works of Samuel Taylor Coleridge, Bollingen
Series, London and Princeton, NJ: Princeton University Press.

—— (1997a) Biographia Literaria, ed. Nigel Leask, London: J. M. Dent and
Sons Ltd.

—— (1997b) Samuel Taylor Coleridge: The Complete Poems, ed. William
Keach, Harmondsworth: Penguin.

—— (2003) Coleridge's Writings, Volume 5: On the Sublime, ed. David
Vallins, Houndmills, Basingstoke: Palgrave Macmillan.

Connor, S. (1989) Postmodern Culture: An Introduction to Theories of the
Contemporary, Oxford: Blackwell.

Cook, J. (1993) 'Paul de Man and Imaginative Consolation in The Prelude',
in Theory in Practice: The Prelude, ed. Nigel Wood, Buckingham
and Philadelphia: Open University Press.

Crawford, D. W. (1974) Kant's Aesthetic Theory, Madison: University of
Wisconsin Press.

Crockett, C. (2001) A Theology of the Sublime, London: Routledge.

Crowther, P. (1989) The Kantian Sublime, Oxford: Clarendon Press.

Crystal, D. (1995) *The Cambridge Encyclopedia of Language*, Cambridge: Cambridge University Press.

Culler, J. (1986) *Saussure*, London: Fontana Press.

de Bolla, P. (1989) *The Discourse of the Sublime: Readings in History, Aesthetics and the Subject*, Oxford: Basil Blackwell.

de Man, P. (1983; 2nd edition) *Blindness and Insight: Essays in the Rhetoric of Contemporary Criticism*, London: Methuen.

—— (1984) *The Rhetoric of Romanticism*, New York: Columbia University Press.

—— (1990) 'Phenomenality and Materiality in Kant', in *The Textual Sublime: Deconstruction and its Differences*, ed. Hugh J. Silverman and Gary E. Aylesworth, Albany: SUNY Press.

Deguy, M. (1993) 'The Discourse of Exaltation: Contribution to a Rereading of Pseudo-Longinus', in *Of the Sublime: Presence in Question*, trans. Jeffrey S. Librett, ed. Jean-François Courtine et al., Albany: SUNY Press.

Derrida, J. (1987) *The Truth in Painting*, trans. Geoffrey Bennington and Ian McLeod, Chicago and London: University of Chicago Press.

Eagleton, T. (1990) *The Ideology of the Aesthetic*, Oxford: Blackwell.

Fairer, D. and Gerrard, C. (eds) (1999) *Eighteenth-Century Poetry: An Annotated Anthology*, Oxford: Basil Blackwell.

Ferguson, F. (1992) *Solitude and the Sublime: Romanticism and the Aesthetics of Individuation*, New York and London: Routledge.

Freeman, B. C. (1995) *The Feminine Sublime: Gender and Excess in Women's Fiction*, Berkeley: University of California Press.

Fry, P. H. (1987) 'The Possession of the Sublime', *Studies in Romanticism*, Vol. 26, No. 2.

Furniss, T. (1993) *Edmund Burke's Aesthetic Ideology: Language, Gender and Political Economy in Revolution*, Cambridge: Cambridge University Press.

Gasché, R. (1990) 'On Mere Sight: A Response to Paul de Man', in *The Textual Sublime: Deconstruction and Its Difference*, ed. Hugh J. Silverman and Gary E. Aylesworth, Albany: SUNY Press.

Goethe, W. (1893) *The Maxims and Reflections of Goethe*, trans. Bailey Saunders, London.

Hamilton, P. (1983) *Coleridge's Poetics*, Oxford: Blackwell.

—— (1999) 'From Sublimity to Indeterminacy: New World Order or Aftermath of Romantic Ideology', in *Romanticism and Postmodernism*, ed. Edward Larrisey, Cambridge: Cambridge University Press.

Hartman, G. (1971) *Wordsworth's Poetry, 1787–1814*, Cambridge, Mass.: Harvard University Press.

Hawkes, D (2003; 2nd edition) *Ideology*, London and New York: Routledge.

Hegel, G. W. F. (1975) *Aesthetics: Lectures on Fine Art*, 2 vols, trans. T. M. Knox, Oxford: Clarendon Press.

—— (1977) *The Phenomenology of Spirit*, trans. A. V. Miller, Oxford: Clarendon Press.

Hertz, N. (1985) *The End of the Line: Essays on Psychoanalysis and the Sublime*, New York: Columbia University Press.

Hipple, W. J. (1957) *The Beautiful, the Sublime, and the Picturesque in Eighteenth-Century British Aesthetic Theory*, Carbondale: Southern Illinois University Press.

Holy Bible: New International Version (2001) London: Hodder and Stoughton.

Hope Nicolson, M. (1959) *Mountain Gloom and Mountain Glory: The Development of the Aesthetics of the Infinite*, Ithaca, NY: Cornell University Press.

Jameson, F. (1991) *Postmodernism, or, The Cultural Logic of Late Capitalism*, London and New York: Verso.

Kant, I. (1960) *Observations on the Feeling of the Beautiful and Sublime*, trans. John T. Goldthwait, Berkeley: University of California Press.

—— (1963) *On History*, trans. L. W. Beck, Indianapolis: Bobbs-Merrill Educational Publishing.

—— (1965) *Immanuel Kant's Critique of Pure Reason*, ed. N. Kemp-Smith, London: Macmillan.

—— (1972) *The Moral Law: Kant's Groundwork of the Metaphysics of Morals*, trans. H. J. Paton, London: Hutchinson University Library.

—— (1987) *Critique of Judgement*, trans. Walter S. Pluhar, Indianapolis and Cambridge, Mass.: Hackett Publishing Company.

Keats, J. (1978) *The Poems of John Keats*, Cambridge, Mass.: Harvard University Press.

Knapp, S. (1985) *Personification and the Sublime: Milton to Coleridge*, Cambridge, Mass.: Harvard University Press.

Kramnick, I. (1977) *The Rage of Edmund Burke: Portrait of an Ambivalent Conservative*, New York: Basic Books.

Kristeva, J. (1982) *Powers of Horror: An Essay on Abjection*, trans. Leon S. Roudiez, New York: Columbia University Press.

Lacan, J. (1979) *The Four Fundamental Concepts of Psychoanalysis*, ed. Jacques-Alain Miller, trans. Alan Sheridan, Harmondsworth: Penguin.

—— (1985) *Écrits: A Selection*, trans. Alan Sheridan, London: Routledge.

—— (1992) *The Seminar of Jacques Lacan*, Book VII, ed. Jacques Alain Miller, *The Ethics of Psychoanalysis*, trans. Dennis Porter, London: Routledge.

Lacoue-Labarthe, P. (1989) 'On the Sublime', in *Postmodernism: ICA Documents*, ed. Lisa Appignanesi, London: Free Association.

Leitch, V. P. (2001) 'Horace', in *The Norton Anthology of Theory and Criticism*, ed. Vincent B. Leitch et al., New York and London: W. W. Norton and Company.

Longinus (1964) *On the Sublime*, ed. D. A. Russell, Oxford: Clarendon Press.

—— (1965) *'Longinus' On Sublimity*, ed. and trans. D. A. Russell, Oxford: Clarendon Press.

—— (1975) *On the Sublime*, trans. William Smith (1739) with an introduction by William Bruce Johnson, Delmar, NY: Scholars' Facsimiles & Reprints.

Lyotard, J.-F. (1984) *The Postmodern Condition: A Report on Knowledge*, trans. Geoff Bennington and Brian Massumi, Manchester: Manchester University Press.

—— (with J. L. Thebaud) (1985) *Just Gaming*, trans. W. Godzich, Manchester: Manchester University Press.

—— (1987) 'The Sign of History', in *Post-structuralism and the Question of History*, ed. Derek Attridge, Geoffrey Bennington, and Robert Young, Cambridge: Cambridge University Press.

—— (1988) *The Differend: Phrases in Dispute*, trans. Georges Van Den Abbeele, Manchester: Manchester University Press.

—— (1989) *The Lyotard Reader*, ed. Andrew Benjamin, Oxford: Basil Blackwell.

—— (1991) *The Inhuman: Reflections on Time*, trans. Geoffrey Bennington and Rachel Bowlby, Cambridge: Polity Press.

—— (1992) *The Postmodern Explained to Children: Correspondence 1982–1985*, trans. and ed. Julian Pefanis and Morgan Thomas, London: Turnaround.

—— (1994) *Lessons on the Analytic of the Sublime*, trans. E. Rottenberg, Stanford, Calif.: Stanford University Press.

Macksey, R. (1997) 'Longinus', in *The Johns Hopkins Guide to Literary Theory and Criticism*, ed. Michael Groden and Martin Kreiswirth http://www.press.jhu.edu/books/hopkins_guide_to_literary_theory/longinus.html.

Maclachlan, I. (ed.) (2004) *Jacques Derrida: Critical Thought*, Aldershot: Ashgate.

Malpas, S. (2003) *Jean-François Lyotard*, London: Routledge.

Marvell A. (1972) *The Poems of Andrew Marvell*, ed. Hugh Macdonald, London: Routledge and Kegan Paul Ltd.

Maxwell, C. (2001) *The Female Sublime From Milton to Swinburne: Bearing Blindness*, Basingstoke: Palgrave Macmillan.

Mellor, A. K. (1993) *Romanticism and Gender*, New York and London: Routledge.

Milbank, J. (2004) 'Sublimity: The Modern Transcendent', in *Transcendence: Philosophy, Literature, and Theology Approach the Beyond*, ed. Regina Schwartz, New York and London: Routledge.

Milton, J. (1980) *The Complete Poems*; ed. B. A. Wright with introduction and notes by Gordon Campbell, London: J. M. Dent & Sons Ltd.

Monk, S. H. (1960) *The Sublime: A Study in Critical Theories in 18th Century England*, New York: Modern Languages Association.

Morrison, T. (1987) *Beloved*, London: Chatto & Windus.

—— (1998) 'Interview' in *Tony Morrison: Beloved*, ed. Carl Plasa, Cambridge, Mass.: Icon Books.

Myers, T. (2003) *Slavoj Žižek*, London: Routledge.

Nancy, J. L. (1993) 'The Sublime Offering', in *Of the Sublime: Presence in Question*, trans. Jeffrey S. Librett, ed. Jean-François Courtine et al., Albany: SUNY Press.

Newman, B. (1990) 'The Sublime Is Now', in *Selected Writings and Interviews*, ed. John P. O'Neill, New York: Alfred A. Knopf.

Paine, T. (1995) *Rights of Man, Common Sense and Other Political Writings*, ed. Mark Philp, Oxford: Oxford University Press.

Parkin-Gounelas, R. (2001) *Literature and Psychoanalysis: Intertextual Readings*, Houndmills, Basingstoke: Palgrave.

Paulson, R. (1983) *Representations of Revolution: 1789–1820*, New Haven: Yale University Press.

Perkins, M. A. (1994) *Coleridge's Philosophy: The Logos as Unifying Principle*, Oxord: Oxford University Press.

Plato (1951) *The Symposium*, trans. W. Hamilton, Harmondsworth: Penguin.

—— (1976) *The Republic*, trans. A. D. Lindsay with introduction and notes by Renford Bambrough, London: J. M. Dent & Sons Ltd.

Radcliffe, A. (1980) *The Mysteries of Udolpho*, Oxford: Oxford University Press.

Readings, B. (1991) *Introducing Lyotard: Art and Politics*, London: Routledge.

Scarry, E. (2000) *On Beauty and Being Just*, London: Duckworth.

Schapiro, B. A. (1983) *The Romantic Mother: Narcissistic Patterns in*

Romantic Poetry, Baltimore and London: Johns Hopkins University Press.

Schiller, F. (1988) *Essays*, ed. Walter Hinderer and Daniel Dahlstrom, New York: Continuum.

Schlegel, F. (1991) *Philosophical Fragments*, trans. Peter Firchow, Minneapolis: University of Minnesota Press.

Sharpe, M. (2002) 'The Sociopolitical Limits of Fantasy: September 11 and Slavoj Žižek's Theory of Ideology', *Cultural Logic* http://eserver.org/clogic/2002/sharpe.html.

Shelley, M. (1985) *Frankenstein or, The Modern Prometheus*, ed. Maurice Hindle, Harmondsworth: Penguin.

Sim, S. (1996) *Jean-François Lyotard*, Hemel Hempstead: Prentice Hall.

Simpson, D. (ed.) (1988) *The Origins of Modern Critical Thought: German Aesthetics and Literary Criticism from Lessing to Hegel*, Cambridge: Cambridge University Press.

Sophocles (1947) *The Theban Plays*, trans. E. F. Watling, Harmondsworth: Penguin.

Spectator (1965) Vol. III, ed. Donald F. Bond, Oxford: Clarendon Press.

Stevens, W. (1984) *Collected Poems*, London: Faber and Faber Ltd.

Sweet, N. (1994) 'History, Imperialism, and the Aesthetics of the Beautiful: Hemans and the Post-Napoleonic Moment', in *At the Limits of Romanticism: Essays in Cultural, Feminist, and Materialist Criticism*, ed. Mary A. Favret and Nicola J. Watson, Bloomington and Indianapolis: Indiana University Press.

Trott, N. (1998), 'The Picturesque, the Beautiful and the Sublime', in *A Companion to Romanticism*, ed. Duncan Wu, Oxford: Blackwell.

Weigel M. (2001) 'Terrorism and the Sublime, or, Why We Keep Watching' http://tvnews3.televisionarchive.org/tvarchive/html/article_mw1.html.

Weiskel, T. (1976) *The Romantic Sublime: Studies in the Structure and Psychology of Transcendence*, Baltimore and London: Johns Hopkins University Press.

Wlecke, A. O. (1973) *Wordsworth and the Sublime*, Berkeley: University of California Press.

Wood, T. E. B. (1972) *The Word 'Sublime' and Its Context 1650–1760*, The Hague: Mouton.

Wordsworth, W. (1984) *The Oxford Authors: William Wordsworth*, ed. Stephen Gill, Oxford: Oxford University Press.

Wu, D. (ed.) (1998) *Romantic Women Poets: An Anthology*, Oxford: Blackwell.

Yaeger, P. (1989) 'Toward a Female Sublime', in *Gender and Theory:*

Dialogues on Feminist Criticism, ed. Linda Kauffman, Oxford: Blackwell.

Žižek, S. (1989) *The Sublime Object of Ideology*, London: Verso.

—— (1999) *The Žižek Reader*, ed. Elizabeth Wright and Edmund Wright, Oxford: Blackwell.

—— (2000a) *The Fragile Absolute; or Why the Christian Legacy is Worth Fighting For*, London: Verso.

—— (2000b) *The Art of the Ridiculous Sublime: On David Lynch's Lost Highway*, Washington, DC: Walter Chapin Simpson Center for the Humanities

—— (2002) *Welcome to the Desert of the Real: Five Essays on September 11 and Related Dates*, London: Verso.

—— (2003) 'Not a Desire to Have Him, But to Be Like Him', *London Review of Books*, Vol. 25, No. 16.

INDEX

Related titles from Routledge

Adaptation & Appropriation
Julie Sanders

the NEW CRITICAL IDIOM

From the apparently simple adaptation of a text into film, theatre or a new literary work, to the more complex appropriation of style or meaning, it is arguable that all texts are somehow connected to a network of existing texts and art forms.

Adaptation and Appropriation explores:

- multiple definitions and practices of adaptation and appropriation
- the cultural and aesthetic politics behind the impulse to adapt
- diverse ways in which contemporary literature and film adapt, revise and reimagine other works of art
- the impact on adaptation and appropriation of theoretical movements, including structuralism, post-structuralism, post-colonialism, postmodernism, feminism and gender studies
- the appropriation across time and across cultures of specific canonical texts, but also of literary archetypes such as myth or fairy tale.

Ranging across genres and harnessing concepts from fields as diverse as musicology and the natural sciences, this volume brings clarity to the complex debates around adaptation and appropriation, offering a much-needed resource for those studying literature, film or culture.

Hb: 0-415-31171-3
Pb: 0-415-31172-1

Available at all good bookshops
For ordering and further information please visit:
www.routledge.com

Related titles from Routledge

The Singularity of Literature
Derek Attridge

'Wonderfully original and challenging.'
J. Hillis Miller

Literature and the literary have proved singularly resistant to definition. Derek Attridge argues that such resistance represents not a dead end, but a crucial starting point from which to explore anew the power and practices of Western art.

In this lively, original volume, the author:

- Considers the implications of regarding the literary work as an innovative cultural event
- Provides a rich new vocabulary for discussions of literature, rethinking such terms as invention, singularity, otherness, alterity, performance and form
- Argues the ethical importance of the literary institution to a culture
- Demonstrates how a new understanding of the literary might be put to work in a "responsible", creative mode of reading

The Singularity of Literature is not only a major contribution to the theory of literature, but also a celebration of the extraordinary pleasure of the literary, for reader, writer, student or critic.

Hb: 0-415-33592-2
Pb: 0-415-33593-0

Available at all good bookshops
For ordering and further information please visit:
www.routledge.com

Related titles from Routledge

Genre and Hollywood
Steve Neale

Genre and Hollywood provides a comprehensive introduction to the study of genre. In this important new book, Steve Neale discusses all the major concepts, theories and accounts of Hollywood and genre, as well as the key genres which theorists have written about, from horror to the Western. He also puts forward new arguments about the importance of genre in understanding Hollywood cinema.

Neale takes issue with much genre criticism and genre theory, which has provided only a partial and misleading account of Hollywood's output. He calls for broader and more flexible conceptions of genre and genres, for more attention to be paid to the discourses and practices of Hollywood itself, for the nature and range of Hollywood's films to be looked at in more detail, and for any assessment of the social and cultural significance of Hollywood's genres to take account of industrial factors.

In detailed, revisionist accounts of two major genres - film noir and melodrama - Neale argues that genre remains an important and productive means of thinking about both New and old Hollywood, its history, its audiences and its films.

Hb: 0-415-02605-9
Pb: 0-415-02606-7

Available at all good bookshops
For ordering and further information please visit:
www.routledge.com